Antiquity Comes Full Circle

by

Easton Hamilton

A TRIBUTE

All three books in this trilogy (of which this is the second) are dedicated to my late, beloved wife, Deborah Hamilton.... She left such a beautiful legacy, far more than I can document here. I will always be grateful to her for her unwavering support, love and friendship over twenty-seven years.

During the last seven and a half years of her life, when Deborah knew she was dying, she became a beautiful example of how to live life whilst knowing death was inevitable. She spent those years using the challenge of her experience to uplift and inspire others, even though she was the one facing a terminal illness. During this time, in fact, within hours of her final moments, Deborah told me to be aware that there was 'something' I was going to need to do. She told me that I wouldn't need to look for it because it would come and find me and that our journey together, especially the final chapter, would be invaluable in helping me to complete that something. I now know that this trilogy (which includes: Science... The New God? and Synergy: the cure for all ills) is part of the task she was referring to and that the rest of this revelation is still quietly unfolding and will come to fruition soon.

Deborah, I want to take this opportunity to thank you for the courage, dignity and grace that you exemplified in life and especially as you were meeting your end. Through the way you lived you taught me how to embrace life and also how to meet death. You also taught me how to be peaceful, stable and content in the face of difficulty; you always did this with such humour and a warm, enigmatic smile. I will keep your legacy with me and endeavour to live my life inspired by those values and virtues.

The beautiful foundation you laid for our children has ensured they continue to blossom. They are both fragrant flowers in the garden of life. There are not enough words to reflect my love, admiration and respect for you. This work, which is an attempt to expand hearts and minds, has been done in part to honour the way you lived your life and the pursuit of truth which was so sacred to you. I hope it will do your memory justice. Thank you for the example of your honesty, courage and integrity. Peace be with you always.

In love and eternal friendship
Easton xx

CONTENTS

PREFACE

In this book I will try to pay homage to many of the great minds and traditions from the East that have been responsible for creating the foundations on which the modern world sits. One could be forgiven for thinking that the developed world got here solely on the strength of its own endeavour, and it is fair to acknowledge that a lot of effort and ingenuity is responsible for the West's many achievements. However, it's also fair to say that without the enormous contribution of the East, the modern world as we know it simply wouldn't exist. The whole of the modern world is built on mathematical concepts. Nothing in our world would work without those. They are the primary building blocks for all our technological advancements, from the mobile telephone to the vast satellites orbiting the earth. The progress we have in so many ways taken for granted, has relied on the genius of mathematics. Its wonderful contribution to the journey of mankind has made its way from India and through the Middle East before eventually landing in Europe. If the Indians had not come up with the number zero, the incredible influence and magic of mathematics simply couldn't have created the foundation that underpins the modern world.

As you take this historical excursion through the eastern continents and dynasties I hope you too will be humbled by the many insights and wisdom you will discover and collect along the way. It is quite staggering to 'listen in' to the thoughts and ideologies of many of the eastern philosophers and great thinkers and to see how very advanced they were in their understanding and interpretations of life. I think, like me, you will appreciate that so much of what was said hundreds of years before Christ is still relevant today, hence the title of this book.... Antiquity has certainly come full circle.

Despite our progress there is something missing at the heart of modernity. I think that the 'something' is spiritual in nature. By spiritual I mean a morality, a code of conduct or set of values underpinning our motives and intentions. Pursuing progress for its own sake is, in my opinion, a 'soul-less' endeavour. This is why so much of what we have achieved has not brought us peace of mind and/or made us any happier. Look around you: are you really happier because you have more gadgets and things? Have you found contentment in the endless pursuit of kudos, status and material possessions? I think if you are honest with yourself the answer is no. My experience of working intensively within the public, private, voluntary, health, education and statutory sectors, is that no matter the context or environment I have been exposed to, the same problems keep turning up with different names! Progress has not brought us happiness and it is my proposition to you that without values and ethics to underpin how we live and what we do in our lives, progress alone will never bring peace of mind and contentment. This is why I think we need to look to the past to inform our future. This is not about living in the past because there is no future in that. This is actually about learning the lessons that our past has come to teach us and then taking the best of those lessons with us into what I believe would certainly be a better future.

"Life can only be understood looking backwards but it must be lived looking forwards."

Friedrich Wilhelm Nietzsche (1844-1900)

As you read this book, decide for yourself whether many of the ideas, values, concepts and principles only belong to yesterday and are therefore best consigned to history.... or whether they would serve us just as well today, if we had the humility to learn from our ancestors? This is a decision you will have to make for yourself. I hope you will enjoy the many twists and turns of this wonderful story and be inspired to take the next leg of the journey, which is where you will be invited to ask yourself arguably the most difficult question: are you being the very best you can be?

The final book in the trilogy is Synergy: the cure for all ills. This is the climax of the story I have attempted to tell. It is a story that I hope will have you reaching for virtue above knowledge. Of course knowledge is precious: where would we be without it? But if knowledge takes us away from virtue, then can it be said to have any real value? 'Synergy: the cure for all ills' will attempt to show you how to convert all the information contained in 'Science... The New God?' and indeed this book, into a workable formula that will help you maximise your potential. So, if by the time you've read this work and you've been inspired to read on, then I believe the final book in the sequence will be the most potent of the three.... Enjoy!

ACKNOWLEDGMENTS

Although I would not have chosen many of the things that have befallen me in this life, the truth is that I owe a huge debt to the enormous challenges I've undergone and the many mistakes that I've made along the way. They have been my best tutors. They have faithfully held up a mirror for me to look into. Some of the time this has been painful and difficult and at other times it has been insightful and inspiring. Both sets of experiences have been priceless because without them my mind would not have been driven to better understand the complexities of the human condition. My experience has forced me to ask the difficult questions that I believe at some point pass through all of our minds. The gift of a probing mind has served me well because I've been able to look at and confront those things that I have not liked in others, the world and most of all in myself and in facing my own darkness I have increasingly found the light.

I would like to take this opportunity to thank my Mother because in spite of my faults and failings she has always encouraged me, believed in me and taught me, through her guidance, support and her love. My Father has also been a wise counsel and friend when I've needed to honestly scrutinise myself. They have both taught me the power of kindness and generosity and that giving is its own reward…. Thank you both for everything you've done for me - I owe you my life.

Special thanks go to Jo Kilburn who has, through her unwavering support, hard work and friendship over the last 20 years, made this trilogy possible. At every step she's contributed her energy, time and enthusiasm and this project simply wouldn't have happened without her. I also need to thank my family, especially my children, Rebecca and Earl, as well as my sister-in-law, Tracy Falconer, all of whom have unconditionally supported and believed in me, through the good times and especially the bad. They have been such wonderful companions. Special mention goes to Elaine Jackson and Judith Madeley, who've faithfully walked by my side now for many years and have both helped to make Reach an organisation built on conscience and integrity. I am eternally grateful to them for their love, consistent support and friendship.

I also owe a great debt to Rashna Walton and Jocelyne Ansorge. They have also both, at different points over the years, lent me their eyes and intellects to enhance this and other written works I have produced. Thank you both for your invaluable contribution and friendship.

Finally I want to thank the literally thousands of clients who have allowed me to be their special companion on their unique journeys into the self. Each and every one of you has added to me in some way. You've helped me to develop understanding and insights beyond my capacity, to discover levels of empathy and compassion I didn't know I had; you've kept me driving down a path looking for sustainable solutions; you have enabled me to find things that really work and truly last. You all know who you are and I hope by recognising your own virtues and qualities you'll have some idea of the gifts you've given to me.

I hope everyone who chooses to take this excursion will find it rewarding and enriching.

Easton Hamilton

"Gratitude is not only the greatest of virtues but the parent of all others."

Cicero (106BC – 43BC)

EASTON HAMILTON

INTRODUCTION

As promised, I am now going to tell the eastern story - at least some strands of the great influence eastern philosophy and culture have had on world history. One could be forgiven for thinking the eastern story is the tale of another planet because in so many ways it bears little resemblance to that of the western world, and although this is still true, there is no doubt that things are changing as the East is busy replicating so much of the western manifesto. The ascent of science continues to dominate world thinking and world perspective, however there is still a significant metaphysical heritage to be found in the East worthy of our attention.

As discussed in 'Science: The New God?' the western world largely ignored the voices of Descartes, Hume, Kant and others who encouraged an 'inward looking habit' – a conscience that is not seduced by the pull, the magic and the promise of the scientific thrust. There was no such debate in the East as the great minds from long before Christ spoke almost in unison: the message was that 'truth', if it could be understood at all, could be best understood by exploring the inner universe and not simply the outer one. This largely shared concept of introspection did not mean there was no difference of opinion or lack of diversity. On the contrary, there are vast differences in the various strands of eastern thinking. In fact the range of thought and spiritual literature is staggering, including as it does: the Upanishads, the Vedas, the Bhagavad Gita, the Analects, the Tao Te Ching, the Koran, the Doctrine of the Mean, to name a few, covering all aspects of the human experience. For those who want to delve more deeply, there is a lifetime of stimulating material largely pointing its students in one direction, that is, inwards. Whilst the West was, and probably still is, predominantly consumed with material expression, the message echoing out of the eastern continents was simple: become a disciple of 'The Way' (Tao). Whether in Korea, Japan, China or India, the eastern intellects and hearts have been singing from the same hymn sheet. The song being sung is: "until we become disciples of life's majesty we are unlikely to find peace, joy and harmony". In other words, all things are best understood by becoming a student of life; true science (knowing) comes from honouring one's teacher. And could there be a greater teacher than life itself?

This is why the journey of enlightenment and bliss that Buddha, Lao Tzu, Patanjali, Confucius, Mahāvīra and others spoke of requires something we seem to have lost… humility. Without humility one becomes blinded by arrogance, vanity and conceit. Is this not an accurate reflection of where we find ourselves right now? To me it seems clear that the ego is and has been running rampant across the planet, deceiving and seducing us along the way. It has promised us greatness and unlimited powers: power over nature, mastery of the universe and ultimate knowledge. Yet we've failed to see that whilst the ego has kept some of its promises we are probably further away from the 'truth' about ourselves because of it. The moral and ethical emphases that have been treasured for centuries in the East have little power in the developed world and are sadly fading even in the East. Humility is largely seen more as a weakness than as a sign of greatness and certainly isn't the average person's preoccupation.

"The attainment of wealth and honour through the violation of one's character is no attainment at all."

Confucius (551-479 B.C.)

Wouldn't we be better off if science and spirituality were not competitors but could become allies? Do they not each offer unique gifts and insights that we need? Isn't the world best understood by explaining both the inner and outer universes? Which is the most important - Science or Spirituality? Can we not have both? I think the best of both is essential and the new infant, neurotheology (the newly developed study where science and spirituality meet), is one discipline that is actively supporting that position. It's time we dared to think differently about our realities and replaced ego and competition with humility and co-operation!

Let us see what else the eastern schools of thought could, if we were willing to listen, teach us....

CHAPTER 1: THE BIRTH OF SPIRITUALITY

Mother India?

In 1921 British and Indian archeologists discovered the ruins of an ancient city in Punjab called Harappa. It helped to clarify that India was indeed the Mother of Civilization. This discovery showed that civilization was not a product of the classical world; Greece, Rome and Ancient Egypt. In fact long before these civilizations emerged, around 3,500 BC, there was a thriving metropolis (of up to 50,000 citizens) on the banks of the River Indus. There was in fact a whole series of cities along the banks of the Indus known as the Indus cities (with a total population of around 200,000 citizens). From the archeological and meteorological evidence we have it appears that the demise of these great cities and clearly sophisticated civilizations was brought about by climate change leading to a shifting of the course of the rivers which in turn forced a massive migration.

The Vedas (ancient Indian scriptures) tell us that around 1500 BC language and literature are born in the north of India, leading to a movement from the exclusively oral tradition of the passing on of wisdom (which in some places still continues) to writing down such jewels in the new language, Sanskrit. This has further helped us to construct a picture of the events of that time.

On February 2nd 1786 William James, a Welsh judge, having persuaded a Brahmin priest and scholar to teach him Sanskrit (a rare departure from the secret passing on of spiritual teachings of that time) made an interesting discovery. In his lecture to the Asiatic Society he pointed out the similarities between Sanskrit, Latin and Greek. He was even able to find similarities with the English and Welsh languages! His discovery helped to establish a principle accepted by most linguists that these three primary languages of the time sprang from a common source. That source is said to be the 'Aryans' (which means 'the civilized'), who entered India in 1500 BC according to the Rig Veda and the archeological evidence available. They brought their language and new Gods and settled in the Valley of the Indus, also along the Indus river. They then started the next civilization, which succeeded the original Harappan civilization. It appears that they migrated due to climate change (so much of history seems to be shaped by climate change and natural disaster) from central Asia (Turkmenistan) into Iran and India. It also appears that they then went on to dominate and shape the evolution of India for the next one thousand years. This brings us to the time of the fifth century BC, a time that could be called the 'birth of conscience and ethics'. In India, China, Greece (Thales, Socrates, Plato), Israel (Old testament prophets) a host of thinkers emerged: rationalists, atheists and skeptics rebelling against what had gone before! History is keen to tell us the story of the conquerors and those who waged wars: Alexander, Napoleon, Hitler etc....but what about the peace tellers? Why do they not get the same press? Is it our nature to dramatize and catastrophize? Is peace so unattractive that history constantly favours the drama and impact of war? Although we have to acknowledge the part war plays because so much of history has been shaped by it, for the sake of balance, I think it's also important to underline the part that the peace tellers have played....

Giants of the East

Just as the western world is filled with a plethora of great minds, geniuses and giants, the eastern world is more than able to match those who have been considered pivotal in shaping human thinking, broadening our understanding and perspective. Amongst the greats are some who will be familiar to many in the West, such as: Buddha (India), Confucius (China), Mohammed (Arabia), Guru Nanak (India); Patanjali (India). There are many more whose impact has been huge and who are probably not known. Here are a few worthy of mention: Rabia al-Adawiyya (she was born in Iraq and pivotal in the emergence of Sufism), Al-Kindi (he was born in Iraq, described as the philosopher of the Arabs), Wŏnhyo (he was born in Korea, known as the founder of Korean Buddhism), Yi T'oegye (born in Korea, influenced by Confucius, he sought integration between philosophical theory and practice), Shōtoku Taishi (born in Japan, the Crown Prince, credited with leading Japan into political unity and cultural greatness), Hōnen (he was born in Japan and is credited for emphasizing 'mindfulness' as being the way),

Mahāvīra (born in India, a key character of the Jain religion), Bādarāyana (born in India, described as the 'teacher of teachers' of what are known as the Sacred Sciences). This is not a definitive list by any stretch of the imagination but it begins to highlight the extent to which the eastern contribution to world history has not been sufficiently valued and celebrated as these individuals are not widely known. This work hopes to go some way in giving respect to the important voices and messages of the East.

The Birth of Spirituality?

In 'Science: The New God?' I alluded to the difficulty of defining the moment when science became a force to be reckoned with because this is a matter of differing opinions. However, generally the moment when Galileo, in 1609, looked through the telescope and saw the moon, is considered the birth of modern science. It is equally challenging to pinpoint the birth of spirituality because this too has many contenders. Dependent on what view of history you take, there are different moments that might be chosen with regards to the birth of spirituality and religion. Is it the birth of Christ, Buddha reaching enlightenment, Confucius writing the Analects or the great writings of the unknown philosophers and teachers compiled under the title of the Upanishads? As all of these events have had a significant impact on philosophy, the evolution of society, culture and world history.

It's worth pointing out though that Confucius, Buddha, Lao Tzu (who was an elder contemporary of the former, who is said by some to have taught Buddha) and the great collections of 'secret teaching' known as the Upanishads were all unfolding their influence on the planet around about the same time, some four hundred to six hundred years before Christ. And so that 'collective influence' might be described as the 'moment of conception' - the point at which the 'spiritual sperm' entered the 'egg of man's consciousness' and the divine enquiry begins its varied and industrious life. It's at this point we will begin our exploration....

The Sperm Meets the Egg

Confucius was born in 551 BC in the state of Lu (now Shantung Province in China). He lived in poverty and was raised just by his mother as his father died when he was only three years old. By the time he was fifteen he set his mind to becoming a scholar. However, after marrying he spent a short period as the Chief of Police in the Department of Justice as he also had political ambitions and hoped to spread his ideas by influencing the existing social consciousness but he soon realized this was not the way to achieve his aims. So he resigned and devoted himself to teaching. For a while he travelled through China with some of his students spreading his ideas about Ren (Pronounced jen) – human heartedness, which he believed to be the highest virtue and the ultimate goal of education but his concepts at the time were largely rejected. However, people were impressed by Confucius' integrity, honesty and particularly by his pleasant personality and enthusiasm. Over three thousand people came to study under him and over seventy became well-established scholars. As a consequence of his impressive personality and philosophy his disciples, over the subsequent centuries, achieved what Confucius had not been able to achieve in his own lifetime, namely getting his ideology nationally recognized. By the time of the second century AD during the Han dynasty, his ideas had won national approval and were embraced by the culture at large. He became honoured as 'The Ultimate Sage Teacher'. Since then his ideas have been taught not only to the traditionally educated Chinese, but also to students in other Asian countries such as Singapore, Korea and Japan. He spent the greater part of his life editing what have come to be known as the 'Confucian Classics' including such books as: The Book of Poetry, The Book of History and the Yi Jing (I Ching) – the Book of changes.

Although he had failed in his limited pursuit to become a political figure there is no doubt his career as an educator and teacher was a tremendous success. His influence has been such that he is considered by the majority to be the most significant figure in Chinese history.

His whole philosophy centered around one concept, the 'primacy of the human heart'. Confucian philosophy revolves around Ren – human heartedness. Although there have been some scholarly disputes about its exact translation, it is clear that Confucius was talking about love. His definition of love was not that of the romantics; impulsive and instinctive. Nor was it the love of God or God's love for humanity. It was quite specific; it was a natural humanistic love, based upon spontaneous feelings, which are able to be cultivated further through education. He saw Ren as a feeling that separated us from other forms of biological beings. Confucius did not see Ren as inborn but as a kind of moral insight resulting from an ethical education and a life experience that provides a reliable evaluation of life. For him it depended on Li (practice of right behavior or moral habits), the attainment of knowledge and Yi (righteousness or proper character). Only then could one develop the 'intuition' to act according to the situation. Confucius famously said, "He who does not know Li (right behaviour) cannot establish himself (attain self-realization)". He saw knowledge and then the practice of Li as the path to human perfection. There has been some debate about the 'fixed' nature of Confucius' position suggesting he simply advocated a return to antiquity but the Analects (a collection of Confucius' notes and quotations) clearly show that he regarded Li as changing through time. For him, change was both inevitable and necessary and was therefore unavoidable. What he really argued for was a form of change that was not disruptive or violent, and was therefore gradual and harmonious. This is Li but it is the adoption of Yi (which he saw as a higher governing principle) – righteousness or proper character that ensured the application of Li in all contexts. This application of Li would then create a peaceful world. A peaceful world is the ultimate goal of Confucianism as summed up by a passage in the book Da Xue (Ta Hsüeh: The Great Learning) which says: 'When the personal life is cultivated, the family will be regulated; when the family is regulated, the state will be in order; and when the state is in order there will be peace throughout the world. From the Son of Heaven down to the common people, all must regard cultivation of their personal life as the root or foundation'.

So we can see self-realization is considered the foundation of peace and order. This concept underpins all his other beliefs and teachings, which we'll come back to later but for now, let's look at the other influences which arguably shaped the birth of spirituality.

The Upanishads date of composition is around six hundred to four hundred years before Christ. This is the work of many unknown Indian philosophers and scholars. The word Upanishad gives us some understanding of this majestic text. The word breaks down into three parts Up (near), ni (down) and shad (to sit). The prose and poetic contents of the Upanishads are based on the act of 'sitting down near' or at the feet of a teacher, who in dialogue with the pupil examines the fundamental issues of existence. This personal face-to-face discussion/tuition with the wise also tells the story of the 'secret oral teaching' passed down through the generations. The Sanskrit texts that emerge from this oral wisdom tradition of many anonymous sages represent the discussions/dialogues of diverse priestly schools all united in their quest for satyāya satyam (the reality of reality). There are thirteen works that are described as the Principal Upanishads from this period and a collection of two hundred other works also called the Upanishads, which came later, mostly during the medieval period. The Principal Upanishads, which serve as the broad foundation of India's philosophical thought, are also known as Vedānta. As Vedānta, the Upanishads offer a revolutionary shift of focus in ancient Hinduism. The shift caused by the Vedānta sees a turning away from the hymnology of Gods and Goddesses to an earnest search for one universal reality, that is 'constant' within the ever-changing. This is the primary focus of this text: to seek to discover the 'unchanging'. This hope is expressed in the prayer of the Brihadaranyaka Upanishad : "From the unreal lead me to the real, from the darkness lead me to the light, from death lead me to immortality".

The beautiful narratives of the Upanishads advise on inward

journeys, deep into the self rather than on outward movement towards the world. There is an intense preoccupation with human consciousness and all that flows from the act of self-reflection. This extensive collection of poetry and prose tells us that the enlightened person realizes that through self-knowledge, the knowledge of the whole universe is captured. The belief being that self-knowledge moves a person ever deeper into the Absolute. In other words, to truly 'know' Truth is to 'become' truth. The Upanishadic ideology clearly emphasizes that it is possible for *every* person to achieve what Christianity said, six hundred years later, *only* Christ could achieve - perfect humanity (divinity in human life).

It is worth noting that the more one explores and examines the eastern philosophies, the more one discovers that many of the ethics, values and principles that underpin human understanding were first conceived in the East. For example: the teachings of Socrates, Plato, Aristotle and even Christ that would influence so much of western/European evolution, right up to the present day, are first articulated in the East. Concepts such as: compassion, non-violence, mindfulness, kindness, truthfulness, charity etc...are first spoken about in China and India by Confucius, Buddha, Lao Tzu, and Patanjali and the masterpiece that is the Upanishads is also part of the spiritual/moral/ethical foundation first seen in the East. This eastern influence is not confined to our past. If, for instance, we look at just the birth and evolution of psychoanalysis, which started with Freud and now has countless modern manifestations, we can still hear the echoes of eternity dressed up as new ideas, ringing loudly in our ears. The concept of the ego, id and superego are first referred to, albeit in a different language, in the Upanishads; later references can also be found in the Bhagavad Gita. In fact, there are numerous references that can be cited in Jainism, Sufism, Islam and Buddhism, long before the time of Freud and his contemporaries. And yet the eastern contribution seems not to have been adequately commended for such concepts and ideas. I will come back to this point later but let us continue to tell this important tale of conception...

Siddhārtha Gautama is another important character in this story. He's better known to the world as Buddha. Buddha was born in India in 563 BC. He was one of a handful of human beings who mirrored the highest human qualities throughout his life. It was his noble character, penetrating intellect, love of humanity and transcendent wisdom that led to his adoration by millions. Buddha was a philosopher, a doctor of the mind and he became a religious leader. The religion founded in his name started in India, spread all over Asia and eventually throughout the world. Its impact remains after more than twenty-five centuries. Buddhism is such a tolerant and gentle teaching that not a single example can be given of blood being shed in order to convert others to its ideology and principles. How unique, when so many wars have been waged in the name of religion!

India in Buddha's time was undergoing social transformation and the long established Vedic religion had degenerated into mere ritualism. The rigid caste system was born with all its inequalities and disadvantages. The 'new' intellectual striving was being articulated through the Upanishads. The philosophy of the Upanishads spoke of an ultimate reality underlying the material world, an absolute power and intellect, transcendent, pure consciousness, known as

Brahman. It also stated that the essence of the human being was that of a pure consciousness, this was described as Ātman. Brahman (God) and Ātman (soul) were seen as one. However, through illusion and ignorance (maya) Atman gets associated with the body and ends up living the 'limited' life of a human being. The right and wrong actions committed by the person form his karma, good actions bearing good fruit, bad actions further imprisoning Atman. The law of karma states that one's next existence is influenced by the last: we reap what we sow. Karma is therefore intertwined with reincarnation. This relationship is known as samsāra. The ultimate goal is to escape samsāra and achieve moksha (final freedom – liberation). There were many bright minds, young, energetic seekers, who were not satisfied with the Upanishadic philosophy. Although it was a new, refreshing departure from the Vedic ritualism for them it did not go far enough. Buddha belonged to this group.

Buddha was born as Siddhārtha, his family name was Gautama. His father was a Chieftain and King and Buddha was born as a Prince and lived a life of luxury in which he was sheltered from the trials of ordinary life. In line with tradition, his father arranged his marriage to Yasodharā who bore him a son, Rāhula. His father's attempts to shield him from the harsh realities of life as he prepared him to become a king did not succeed. On one of his rare trips outside the palace, Buddha noticed an old man, a sick man and a corpse. He realized that the infirmities of old age, the pain of sickness and the certainty of death highlight the inevitable sufferings of life. He began to wonder if there was a way of life that could conquer suffering and lead to tranquility. This question was to become the driving force of his life, to such an extent that he renounced his family and his kingdom and became a wandering ascetic (monk). At first he pursued the path of yogic meditation, which enabled him to achieve elevated states of consciousness but this was not enough for him. He went on to practice severe austerities such as prolonged fasting, suspension of breathing etc. So severe were his practices that he came close to death but his questions had not been answered. Finally, he resolved to take a seat under the Bodhi tree, facing east and not to rise until he attained enlightenment. It is said that on the night of the full moon he ascended through four stages of trance and during the last few hours of that night he acquired enlightenment (Bodhi) and Gautama became the Buddha (The Enlightened One). He was now thirty-five years old. Buddha had seen the path that leads to the end of all suffering and to liberation (nirvāna). He wondered whether the world was ready for his teaching. He called his path the 'Middle Way'. This is because he rejected both asceticism and hedonism as one-sided extremes. He would spend the next forty-five years (the rest of his life) teaching the 'Middle Way', a doctrine which would come to be known as Buddhism.

This period of history would be incomplete without reference to Lao Tzu. Dates about his birth and death are ambiguous and have become the stuff of legend. He was born in the sixth century BC and is an elder contemporary of Confucius. Although Confucius is often described as the most significant figure in Chinese history, there are those (certainly Daoists) who might argue Lao Tzu is equally worthy of that accolade. He is credited with being Buddha's teacher, an author of many books, a philosopher of amazing intellect and insight. It's worth noting that his most significant work Dao De Jing

(Tao Te Ching) has been the subject of much debate and there are some scholars who wonder if it is indeed his work or was in fact authored by several people. However both the Daoist (Taoist) and Confucian traditions dispute that any ambiguity surrounds Lao Tzu's contribution.

Lao Tzu grew discontent with what was happening in China and left to travel to India. It is at this point that he is said to have met Buddha. He found him sitting under the Bodhi tree. He instructed him over a period of time and is considered pivotal (by Daoists) in helping Gautama to become Buddha (The Enlightened One). There is within the Daoist tradition a book (Hua Hu Ching) that claims to partly record the teaching passed on by Lao Tzu to Buddha. However, this has been considered slanderous by some Chinese Buddhists, ever since it emerged around the third or fourth century AD.

As the text Dao De Jing (Tao Te Ching) rose in importance so did Lao Tzu. He eventually came to be seen by Daoists as a cosmic and divine figure. This relatively small text of eighty-one short chapters, a little over 5,000 Chinese characters, was to have an impact that would resonate not just through the East but eventually the world. Dao basically means: 'the way things do what they do'. It has been shortened to simply 'the way'. It has become arguably the single most important and influential text to ever come out of China. Its unique, poetic style has left it open to countless interpretations over the last two thousand years. Some have described it as a politically subversive document, whilst others have seen it as the ultimate metaphysical transcript. On closer examination of the subsequent interpretations, it seems that the different perspectives and points of view often reveal individual prejudices and agenda rather than honour the relative innocence and beauty of the text. You may want to take a closer look at this for yourselves and make your own minds up about this pivotal work. Lao Tzu's philosophy is a plea to return to infancy, to return to what he described as 'uncarved blocks'. Both the infant and the uncarved block are at the point where they are capable of becoming anything: unlimited possibilities awaiting them.

As we go further we will expand on the evolution and influence of the Upanishads, Buddha, Confucius and Lao Tzu. All four are responsible in different ways for a revolution in thinking and ideology. They have all shaped and moulded the human story and become catalysts for religion triumphing over ritual (blind faith) and developing a new way of seeing the self and how it relates to the cosmos.

It's worth reflecting on what we've discovered so far. Essentially, at this point in the story, some five hundred to six hundred years before Christ, we can see a number of themes emerging in both India and China, influenced by the great minds and works (texts) I've referred to. The primary themes are:

i) **Introspection** – it's clear that all of the substantive philosophies pointed to 'looking inward' in order to find the answers, the 'truth'. Those philosophies did not believe the world could be fully understood by external scrutiny alone.

ii) **Ethics and morality** – in different yet converging ways these philosophies are underpinned by the ideology that one's spiritual endeavour depends on 'right thinking', 'right action' and the 'right treatment' of others. In other words, one couldn't expect to thrive spiritually without a conscience.

iii) **Virtues** – these philosophies also speak of love, compassion, sacrifice, benevolence and kindness to name a few. These are considered the highest attainments of life. They ask the question: what if we've worked life out and yet have no heart, no divinity and character? Where's the benefit in that?

iv) **Humility** – for each one of these philosophies, our egos are considered to be our single biggest obstacle. Until we learn to get out of our own way, our egos will continue to deceive us and as a result encourage us to pursue the wrong things - the limited rather than the unlimited.

So, spirituality was born and offered some clarity about the way forward. However, we should not make the mistake that because there were common denominators that there was a complete unity of ideology. There were clear differences to be found at the time; we can point to even greater ones now, as opinion, interpretation and dogma have altered and affected some of the original concepts and philosophies. I'm going to invite you to take a journey further down the eastern corridors of history so we can see if what currently divides humankind is in fact greater than what unifies us. My proposition is that the great gaping gaps and divisions we can see around the planet largely exist because our focus is far too much on our differences rather than on what binds us.

The Evolution of Spirituality and Religion

The premise I've put forward so far i.e. 'a moment of spiritual conception', by its very definition may appear to diminish what spiritual knowledge and understanding existed before that moment and could also mask other important, relevant factors in the same time period. I can only say that this is the nature of any investigative process. By focusing on what we believe to be the salient points we are bound to omit things that others might see as relevant. However, I don't believe this diminishes the value of what I am putting forward here because my aim is to simply invite you to think in a more expansive way, to think outside the box, and not be limited by the constraints of the way history is often served up through our educational systems. Having made this point I want to proceed for the sake of balance to acknowledge other important personalities and texts that played some part in the evolution of spirituality and some of the religious traditions that followed as a result.

Some of the Giants of the Past

Mozi's (Mo Tzu) 470 BC – 391 BC: his contribution to the great planetary shifts of that era had some strong similarities to Confucius' but there were also clear differences. One of his core ideas was: benevolence directed to everyone. For Mo Tzu, to love everyone results in the greatest benefit to oneself and to others. He also believed in the Will of Heaven (God), a magnanimous universal force that rewarded our good actions but punished those who persisted in their unfriendly and hurtful actions. The Mohist tradition derived from Mo Tzu's work stated that one should mirror in their actions the Will of Heaven, with gratitude for its countless gifts seen as the highest endeavour. Mo Tzu criticized a number of Confucian ideals and as such was considered the first great heretic of the Confucian tradition. Even though they both believed in unity and a 'principled' society based on the perfection of the individual, they differed as to the means by which this perfection could be achieved. It is the philosophical tension between the Mohist tradition and Confucianism that led to its eventual demise at the time of the Han Dynasty (206 BC – 220 BC). Mo Tzu's work would not be resurrected until the scholars of the Qing dynasty (1644 AD – 1912) sought to reconstruct the primary texts. Some western scholars were also motivated to study Mohism because of its apparent similarities to Christianity. Mo Tzu's views would go on to influence many of the subsequent philosophical and religious systems and as such, for a time, offered teachings powerful enough to rival Confucianism.

Mahāvīra (birth name Vardhamāna): there is some ambiguity about dates – it is believed he was born 540 BC and died 468 BC. There is no ambiguity though about his contribution. He came slightly after Buddha and was born in North East India. So they were contemporaries and shared some of the same views. This can be seen particularly in their theories about karma, although the Jains' concept of karma is more significantly developed than in either Hinduism or Buddhism. According to the Acaranga Sūtra (the oldest of the Jain texts, dating from the fourth or fifth century BC) Mahavira shared the view that spiritual advancement lies in the avoidance of injury to any life forms and he is said, like Buddha, to have achieved enlightenment, what the Jains call kevala (perfect isolation from all harmful actions). This is a state described as 'blessed conscience' and it is how he acquired the title Mahavira (Great Hero) as he renounced 'normal family life' at the age of 30 and spent over 12 years wandering throughout the Ganges river plain, fasting, meditating, listening and like

Buddha, he too pressed against the boundaries between life and death. This earned him the status of being the twenty fourth Great Teacher of the Jain tradition and the most recent to achieve the state of 'blessed omniscience'. The Jain community is now relatively small, located mainly in Gujarat and western Rajasthan but its message of non-violence endures and has influenced many along the way, from the time of the great Indian King Ashoka - two hundred years before Christ- right through to Gandhi.

Bādarāyana : known in India as the 'Teacher of teachers and the splendour of the sacred sciences'. Dates of his birth and death are unclear. All we can safely say is that he was around in the fifth century and was also part of this period which we are describing as the birth/infancy of spirituality – also known as the Axial Age, a time when the spiritual foundations of humanity were laid by a variety of individual thinkers occupying China, India, Greece, Persia and Palestine. As the founder of the Vedantic system and the creator of systematic theology itself (several centuries before its reputed inaugurator Philo Judaeus of Alexandria 15 BC – 45 AD) he clearly greatly influenced events, especially in India. He is also the author of probably the most commented on text of Hindu Theology, the Brahma Sutras. It's worth noting that Indian religious thought displayed a preoccupation with 'systems' philosophy, from its beginnings in the Vedas, which – dependent on the historical clock you use - is said to go as far back as the fifteenth century BC. Most of this Vedic thought has been passed down in an oral tradition (known as the Rig Veda). It was Badarayana who produced an all encompassing, integrated and articulate text that enabled the vast and diverse texts of the Vedas (largely written in poetry and prose) to be formalized into a coherent 'system', a theology. As a result it generally came to be agreed by Vedantins that reality consisted of three categories: the Absolute (Brahman), the individual soul (Jīva) and material reality (Joda). The Absolute being infinite consciousness, the soul being finite consciousness and physical reality being unconscious. This 'tripartite pattern' was used later by systematicians of other religions such as in the monumental works of Catholic systematics i.e. Aquinas (1225-74), Scotus (1265-1308) and Suārez (1548-1617).

Bādarāyana's theology would go on to underpin and influence almost all philosophy and religious ideology to follow, certainly in India. His primary concepts of a Supreme Being (God) that was pure, constant, infinite and never changing and a Self (soul) made from the same material, also a pure being, however also housing negative attributes, still influences very many religious points of view today. The world of the five elements is then seen as the stage on which this drama of life is played out.

Bhagavad Gita: this is one of the great religious classics and is very relevant to this infancy and developmental period. Its author is said to be Vyāsa but dates pertaining to his birth and death are unknown. We know it was written between the fifth and first centuries BC. The Bhagavad Gita (The Song Sung by the Lord) is arguably the earliest attempt by man to arrive at a comprehensive view of existence. It is part of the great Indian epic, The Mahābhārata. It consists of seven hundred verses divided into eighteen chapters. The most important teaching of the Gita is that of altruism and benevolence. It tells the story of how man can reach his highest point by performing actions that are not motivated by the desire to obtain some personal benefit, but rather by the desire to do his duty (dharma), doing what is right for its own sake. To understand the Gita it is necessary to place it in its religio-philosophical and cultural context. So I'd like to offer you a little background…

The Āryans came to India in 1500 BC and although they brought their own Gods and language (Sanskrit), religious life still largely centered on the Vedas. These holy books guided the spiritual thinking and the lives of the Indian people. By 1000 BC life for many had become unsatisfactory and a pious belief in karma and reincarnation added to a growing pessimism. The notion was born that if one life could be so unsatisfactory and there was an endless chain of death and re-birth, then surely moksha (liberation from life and death) had to be the highest goal? The Upanishads (which are the culmination of the Vedas) developed a philosophy which considers that human suffering is conceived out of the spirit's misidentification with the body and therefore moving away from the 'truth' about the self namely that the self is a spirit made up of the same essence as the Supreme Consciousness (the Absolute). The Gita went further than the Upanishads. Through the dialogue that takes place between Krishna and Arjuna (the two principal characters) a wonderful story of love, devotion, courage, sacrifice and morality is told. The concept of moksha being 'the way' to liberation is added to as Krishna explores three other ways to liberation. They are: knowledge, action and devotion. At first Krishna suggests that devotion is the best of these, followed by action and then knowledge in third place. However, the Gita is a harmonizing doctrine, it prefers both/and to either/or, so Krishna ends by saying that the very best way is to combine all three. As we saw with Bādarāyana's input, where he identifies integration as the best course, here too the Gita points us in this direction!

In order to do justice to its contribution, the Gita would deserve a thesis all of its own but this is not my aim. The Gita has indeed had countless commentaries written by almost all classical Indian philosophers, notably Shankara and Ramanuja and more latterly Indian thinkers Sarvepalli Radhakrishnan, Gandhi and Aurobindo. Since the Gita was translated into English by Charles Wilkins in 1785, it is now available in more than thirty languages and about a thousand individual editions. Sadly we can see that the Gita, like so many other scriptures, treatises and philosophical texts has been interpreted in different ways to suit the argument of the day. For example: Shankara, the first great commentator on the Gita, was a firm advocate that the path of knowledge was the only way to moksha and that action and the path of devotion were merely preparatory to knowledge. Ramanuja on the other hand sees the path of devotion as the highest path and the other two as supplementary. The American Transcendentalist, Henry Thoreau, took another view. He saw the Gita as giving form and structure to the ideal of yogic discipline, which emphasized solitude, chastity and austerity. Gandhi, arguably the greatest apostle of non-violence since Mahāvīra and Buddha, referred to the Gita as his spiritual dictionary, which for many may have seemed strange since the Gita is a dialogue between Krishna and Arjuna taking place on a battlefield with Krishna urging Arjuna to fight. Gandhi saw no conflict between the primary thrust of the Gita and his own position because he interpreted the Gita allegorically. He saw the war being waged in the Gita as the war taking place in the heart of each one of us and so Krishna's advice meant one cannot quit the battlefield of the mind and heart. Instead we must find refuge in discipline, controlling our senses, feelings of attachment and lust. Only then can we find liberation in life. Gandhi was clearly such a man, putting his beliefs very much into action (karma).

I feel Ghandi's interpretation of the Gita as an allegorical work is probably the most helpful and for that reason I will come back to some of the other unique tenets of the Gita later in this book...

The story of the Greeks, Romans and the Egyptians is well told and continues to be. My concern is with the lesser-told tale (in the developed world) of the Great Eastern influences and to continue to explore this we need also to refer to three other influential doctrines that have come out of the Chinese traditions and philosophy....

i) The Spring and Autumn Annals of Master Lu, which are essentially concerned with political philosophy and ethics: The Annals are presumed to have been compiled by Lu Pu-Wei (291BC – 235 BC), some time in the third century BC. The work was written by numerous scholars and is therefore an eclectic philosophical work drawing on various teachings from the Zhou (Chou) dynasty several centuries earlier. The text contains one hundred and sixty chapters, divided into three parts: twelve chronicles, eight observations and six discussions. It is thought the Annals were Lu's attempt to write a definitive text on the art of rulership based on integrity and conscience. Each of these three texts had their shortcomings but it's thought that the three as a whole offered the potential for self-mastery. Some of the areas covered include the notion that a ruler must govern with an attitude of public-spiritedness, that proper timing is of the essence in order to achieve political order, that a ruler cannot afford to blindly follow tradition; that he must respond to present circumstances creatively and with innovation and that the teachings of traditional philosophy should be applied according to the seasons. In fact this work implores the ruler, and therefore his subjects, to maintain a respectful and reciprocal relationship with the environment. One of the defining characteristics of Chinese political philosophy is its commitment to cosmic harmony and the Annals seek to engineer just that.

ii) The Great Learning is a literary work about social philosophy and ethics. It is one of the Confucian Canon called 'The Four Books', the other three being: the Analects of Confucius, the Book of Mencius (Mengzi/Meng Tzu) and the Doctrine of Mean (Zhongyang). Originally it was one chapter in a larger Confucian work, the Book of Rites. The authorship of the Great Learning remains an unanswered question even today. Some scholars believe it was written by Confucius' disciple Zengzi (Tseng Tzu), whilst others think Confucius's grandson, Zi Si (Tzu Ssu) composed this great work. It was written in the third or second century BC. The text has been described through the ages as 'a gateway to virtue' and is considered by many Chinese scholars as an unrivaled philosophical work. It was deemed the most important of 'The Four Books' and its significance is such that it is believed that the subtleties and the depth of the other three works cannot be fully grasped and understood without it. Although many have argued that this is a text primarily for a ruler there are those who quite rightly believe it offers insight and benefit to all. The subjects it covers include: organizing the state, bringing tranquility to the world, establishing a harmonious household and cultivating the self, to name a few. In addition, the Great Learning contains the Confucian educational, moral and political programmes. The text is primarily preoccupied with what it sees as the two inseparable goals of morality: firstly, cultivating the self and secondly, ordering the state or society. It provides a clear map for enhancing one's own goodness and virtue and developing a culture of Ren (love) within humanity. Even today it is still considered the best introduction to Confucianism.

iii) The Doctrine of the Mean was composed between the third and second centuries BC and is another one of the Confucian Canon called the 'The Four Books'. Authorship is again called into question. Again Confucius's grandson (Zi Si – 492-431 BC) is thought to have composed this work. However, if it indeed was produced in the third or second century BC, then as indicated by his lifespan, it was after his time. This work is once again concerned with ethics, as almost all great Chinese works are. However, in addition to the ethical theme, its primary focus is metaphysics. This work concerns itself with the Confucian system of moral metaphysics and the philosophy of moral practice. It has helped shape Chinese civilization for more than 2,000 years. In the process it has, to a large extent, brought together the ideas of Buddhism, Daoism and Confucianism and so has become a bridge between the three philosophies. To further clarify the focus and emphasis of this work it is useful to understand what the word 'Mean' in Chinese translates to. The Chinese word for Mean is Zhong (chung), which literally translates to 'central, unbiased and proper'. The principle idea of Zhong is: 'to do it just right'. The whole phrase in Chinese is 'Zhang Yong'. The Yong means : 'central harmony' or 'the way of'. So the Mean is about the highest human conduct, to endeavour to do things in the 'right' way, in a way that's unbiased and promotes harmony. The foundation on which this highest conduct stands is based on the Confucian metaphysical principle of cosmic unity. That is: heaven and man are inseparable. What heaven imparts to man is called nature. To follow nature is called 'the way' (Dao/Tao). To cultivate 'the way' is called education. Heaven here refers to the non-personal supreme deity or spiritual reality. This is a fundamental belief not only in Confucianism, but also in Chinese Buddhism and Daoism.

All three of these great Chinese texts believe the 'Way of Heaven' resides within us all and although human beings are born with a nature invested in them from heaven, this good nature needs to be cultivated and developed in order for an individual to fulfill his potential. This is radically different from the western view, which has nature on one hand and human beings on the other. The Chinese can't see how these two can be separated. This 'Heaven-and-Human-Way' is described as Cheng (ch'eng), which translates as sincerity, reality or truthfulness. Cheng is the Way of Heaven; it is infinite, unlimited, extensive and deep. Cheng is the process of creativity, the 'active' force working through everything in the universe. The highest aspiration is to embrace Cheng: a person who embraces Cheng is true to his nature and so lives sincerely and truthfully in line with Heaven. He becomes a 'superior person' but does not behave in a superior way and so is truly humble. He exemplifies the Way of the Mean:

wisdom, humanity and courage.

Patanjali : before moving on and taking a closer look at how the spiritual web has spread, influencing millions of people, over tens of hundreds of years, one more character remains, who undoubtedly influenced the infancy of spirituality and whose work continues to do so even today. His name is Patanjali. He was born in India and the dates of his birth and death remain unknown. Estimates range from 200 BC to 400 AD (birth) and 150 BC to 450 AD (death). Meditation is and remains an important aspect of religion in India. It is advocated by: Jainism, Buddhism and Brahmanical Hinduism. Patanjali composed a brief textbook drawing from different schools and traditions in which he summarizes several yogic meditation techniques. This manual has become the standard guide for both the theory and practice of meditation in India. His work is known as the Yoga Sūtras. They are composed in Sanskrit and are divided into four sections: Concentration (Samādhi), Practice (Sādhana), Empowerment (Vibhūtti) and Isolation (Kaivalyam). These four concepts are blended together with a number of key themes. One key theme emphasizes control over the mind. Another involves the cultivation of the ability to become and remain the 'seer' (one's unchanging, true self) and not become embroiled in the 'seen' (the ever-changing dance of matter). When one is able to master the mind and remain in the state of 'pure seeing', then one is said to have achieved isolation (Kaivalyam), to have become free from negative influence (karmateet), also known as absorption in the 'Cloud of Virtue".

In the first section of the text, Patanjali lays out his metaphysical, epistemological and logical premises. He states that thought causes one to stray into the realm of the 'seen' in a variety of ways. By practicing detachment and dispassion thought can be restrained, thus generating the desired state of remaining in the 'seer's true form (reality)'. Patanjali states that the ills of the self and of the world can be cured by adopting a consciousness that distances one from attachment to the 'seen'. Patanjali goes on to explain the activities and awareness required to achieve this sate of detachment from the seen. These include: faith, concentration, mindfulness, wisdom, friendliness, compassion, equanimity, happiness and devoting oneself to the significant meditational ideal. There is some overlap here with Buddhist tenets.

The Yoga Sūtras, like all metaphysical works, go on to talk about the importance of ethics. In this regard the Jain influence can clearly be seen in Patanjali's work as he emphasizes: non-violence, truthfulness, sexual restraint, non-attachment and refraining from greed. The philosophy of karma (the law of cause and effect), like many other eastern traditions is given a pivotal place. In fact, the primary purpose of detachment and remaining anchored as the seer is to become free of the consequences of one's negative actions, to become free of past karma and various sorrows of the world. Patanjali warned of the five afflictions, which are: ego, attraction, aversion, ignorance and clinging to life. For him these were the enemy of those striving for liberation in life (Jīvan-Mukta).

The Yoga Sūtras offer great insight into achieving the yogic state (a state of union) and bliss (happiness beyond the senses). Many of its principles and systems continue to be taught, such as chanting, controlling the breath, physical postures etc. all in the name of remaining in the form of the seer, which is a state of being beyond the realm of the material world and change. Unfortunately the dilution and westernization of some of these practices means the focus and emphasis on remaining the seer (the detached observer) has to a large extent become lost. This is reflected in the significant proliferation of a variety of yogic traditions that have gone on to develop only particular aspects of what Patanjali saw as essential ingredients if one is to ascend to the 'cloud of virtue' and taste the sweetness of bliss.

The following chapter in this amazing story focuses on the next thousand years in which we will see further expansion of spiritual ideals, a unifying of moral values and ethics as well as increasing contradiction about the road to enlightenment. We will also see that although the eastern contribution has many unifying principles it has not been without its conflict and disagreements – many of which still remain today. That said I believe its overriding message of good conduct, the pursuit of peace, balance and harmony, is more relevant today than it ever was. This is because modernity and progress seem to be taking us away from the values, ethics and codes of conduct that antiquity was built on.

Surely, it's time for us to see that progress at any cost is not progress at all!

"Who looks outside dreams; who looks inside wakes."

Carl Jung (1875 - 1961)

CHAPTER 2: 500 BC – 500 AD

The Empire of the Spirit

At the time of Buddha's death the great Persian Empire raided and plundered Greece. A century later the Greeks came looking for revenge. As is often the case in history, war becomes the catalyst for change. On October 1st 331 BC arguably the greatest battle of antiquity was fought in the perennial battleground of Iraq; Europe met Asia. Alexander the Great came to fight the Persians and in a famous historic battle against Darius, King of the Persians, Alexander won and Darius fled. Aristotle, who was Alexander's teacher said at the time: "The Greeks have strength and reason and it's right that they should rule the world". With the words of his teacher ringing in his ears, Alexander continued his mission to conquer. He drove through the Khyber Pass and entered India in 326 BC. Alexander was charmed by India's beauty, diversity and wealth and Greece's love affair with India was established. It was there in the Punjab that Alexander met Chandragupta Mauri – who was initially so impressed with Alexander but who in time would be the one to drive

Alexander's successors out of India, thus establishing an enormous kingdom of his own.

Spirituality and religion in all their various forms were also crossing boundaries and borders on the back of conflict and migration. The closer one looks at the East, particularly in India, the more one can see a melting pot of peoples, cultures, arts, ideas and languages, largely as a result of the movement of people and with that the migration of minds and ideas. This is also true of China, Japan and Korea. Over the thousand-year period from 500 BC to 500 AD much would stay the same in the East and yet there would also be great change. It's important to note that a proper examination of the East shows us that the origins of so much of what we call civilisation are to be found in this part of the world. It seems to me that in our re-telling of history, here in the developed world, we have not properly acknowledged the key contribution made by the East to all aspects of human activity: the arts, language, literature, architecture, technology, philosophy and science. And yet as I go on telling this story I hope you will see for yourself the staggering contribution the East has indeed made to the arts, sciences and philosophy and that it has quite simply changed the face of humankind.

In India's on-going relationship with Greece, the Greek ambassadors in 300 BC were amazed by what they saw. Chandragupta reigned over a land of one hundred and eighteen nations and had created cities of such opulence, with communities that had become mixed over time living harmoniously. He ruled from the imperial city of Patna and was considered by many to be the first great king of India. His method of rulership would become the template for his grandson (Ashoka Maurya), who would take his grandfather's model and go on to rule a vast kingdom of his own for nearly forty years.

Chandragupta, at the height of his powers, renounced his kingdom, in fact he renounced everything in pursuit of Moksha (liberation). He followed a Jain Guru and he starved to death in order to achieve Moksha. But his legacy of proper governance, political order and citizenship would be fulfilled by his grandson: Ashoka Maurya.

Ashoka's rule did not start well. He went on to conquer neighbouring communities and to expand his empire, spilling much blood and taking countless lives along the way. He later regretted his actions and the atrocities he had committed. Over time Ashoka began to see that war was inhumane, a hideous crime and as a result he turned to Buddhism as he felt remorse and sought atonement. His message and his rule became one of non-violence. He resolved to conquer by persuasion alone. It was he who came up with new and original edicts (the first real charter) for human and animal rights. Ashoka created a new ethical way of governing, which had never before been seen. He created an 'Empire of the Spirit' in response to the 'Empire of the Sword'. In his attempt to spread peace and brotherhood he sent ambassadors to the kings of Greece, Syria, Macedonia, North Africa, Babylonia and others, in order to build bridges and spread religious tolerance. Ashoka's principles and values would go on to be part of the Indian story of struggle for divine co-existence. Sadly this struggle continues even today. His philosophy and political ideals were built on a marriage between Buddhism and

Jainism and for a while at least they tamed the raging waters of this vast and diverse nation. Ashoka's 'wheel of law' is still depicted at the centre of the Indian flag, such has been his influence on India's political and moral evolution.

China: The Other Great Giant of the East

During the same period, the other great eastern civilisation, China, was going through similar contradictions. It's important to remember that China too has extensive roots that claim to go back at least twenty three centuries BC. Archaeological excavations that took place between 1929 and 1933 in the ancient Shang capital near AnYang, unearthed about a hundred thousand 'dragon bones'. It was discovered that these bones were inscribed with ancient styles of writing. They were in fact 'oracle bones', used in ancient times for divinistic purposes. Through the decoding and deciphering undertaken by various scholars, China's long legacy was confirmed. The writings (the Oracle Runes) and other artefacts, such as the magnificent bronze urns that were discovered confirmed that the Shang dynasty had been the successors to the Hsia (or Xia) dynasty (considered to be the original dynasty emerging two thousand years before Christ and lasting over 500 years). It is now generally accepted that by 1500 BC these highly gifted people with a long history of development behind them fostered a sophisticated and distinctive culture in north China. By the 11th century BC the Shang dynasty was overthrown by the Chou (or Zhou) dynasty. They were a nomadic tribe from the western regions. The Chou were not innovators, they took much of the Shang dynasty's achievements such as: working with bronze, pottery, textiles and developing the written language and went on to develop them further. This mirrors what was happening in India at around the same time. The Chou also reformed the political system creating a new aristocracy and a large peasant class, which through agriculture supported the economy of the time. Their dynasty struggled over the next three hundred years to create any real political stability. This is reflected in the fact that there were about twenty-five semi-independent states all busily undermining the Chou authority. This was a time of population expansion, significant advances in craftsmanship and the growth of a money economy as well as developments in military techniques. In addition there were significant intellectual advances taking place towards the end of the Chou dynasty from which China's great philosophical traditions emerged. This was the time of Confucius, Lao Tzu and Menicus. Despite all this progress the Chou dynasty staggered along, never really achieving a unified state.

By the fourth century BC the fight between the various states became more virulent and uncompromising. So at the point I referred to earlier as the 'birth of spirituality' (see chapter 1) we can see that war and conflict was taking place at the point that the spiritual revolution was beginning. In fact this period in Chinese history (403 BC to 221 BC) became known as the period of the 'Warring States' as countless battles were fought, and smaller states were swallowed up by their increasingly large and ruthless neighbours. It was the western state of Ch'in that emerged triumphant from this period. Its statesmen rejected the moral political philosophy of Confucius with its gentle emphasis on right behaviour. Instead they adopted the uncompromising outlook of the legalists of the time, who offered the Machiavellian advice that 'the end justified the means', upholding the principle that it was right that the individual should be subordinate to the state. So whilst India, under Ashoka the Great, was creating an 'Empire of the Spirit' to replace the sword, Ch'in rulers were going in the other direction. They systematically set about strengthening the central power of the state. Bureaucracy was introduced, massive irrigation works were carried out by forced labour and the population was pressed into military service. One by one the surrounding states were conquered and swallowed up. By 222 BC King Cheng had accomplished the task of creating a 'centralised' empire, the first of its kind in Chinese history. King Cheng then adopted the title Shih Huang Ti and proclaimed himself ruler of the empire (the first of the great Chinese dynasties). The Ch'in Empire brought about lasting changes that influenced the subsequent course of Chinese history. They introduced standard taxes, standard weights and measures and new laws. They were ruthless in monitoring and controlling the thoughts of the educated classes and are reputed to have burnt philosophical and political literature and books in order to 'mould the minds' of the citizens. In order to maintain their control they improved communications by building (largely by forced labour) an elaborate network of roads and canals. Undoubtedly their greatest achievement, which remains one of the wonders of the world, was building the Great Wall of China. This incredible architectural feat stretches for one thousand five hundred miles along the northern borders of China, from the east coast to the mountain ranges in the Chinese interior. Its purpose primarily was to protect the rich agricultural lands they had captured from the many nomads who might want to encroach on their acquisitions. Ironically, the wall that was built to exclude and protect could not stop the internal melt down of the Ch'in dynasty. The harsh laws, enforced labour and continuous drive for military expansion brought a discontent and resentment from the Chinese people, which eventually led to revolt. By 210 BC Shih Huang Ti died and it wasn't long before the second of the great dynasties of ancient China was formed: the Han dynasty. Its influence went on to shape China's evolution for more than four hundred years (206 BC – 220 AD). In an attempt to gain popular support the early Han emperors repealed the ruthless Ch'in laws, rejected the doctrines of the legalists; and Confucianism was encouraged instead, both as a code of moral behaviour for the individual and as a state religion. During this initial period, great cultural, political and institutional developments took place. Assemblies of scholars gathered to debate constitutional matters, examine ancient writings and texts as well as discuss the economic state of the country. However, the early promise of a less centralised system offering a greater autonomy than the Ch'in dynasty was short-lived. It was clear that governmental control would remain and the feudal privileges that had been restored at the beginning of the Han period were gradually eroded. Also new laws of inheritance divided up large estates and with that the status of the nobles was slowly reduced. In their place a competent civil service was established, based on ability not birth. A meritocracy was born in which those who studied diligently and revered knowledge, especially the Confucian Classics, were rewarded with governmental appointments.

This concept of 'just and ethical' rule spread from the capital of Chang'an (modern Sian), across north and central China, which strengthened Han control. For balance it should be noted that this period was not free from conflict and combat. Although there was further expansion internal uprising and rebellion continued against the Han rulers especially in the south of China. There remained from the time of the Ch'in dynasty some significant and resistant forces that continued to defy the Han rulership. In fact they were so resistant that they remained semi-independent until the time of the T'ang dynasty (618 – 907 AD).

The greatest threat to the Han empire came from the north, from the various nomadic tribes like the Hsiung-nu, Yuch-chih and Turgis. These tribes were a constant threat to the Han dynasty's desire for internal control and continuing expansion of its borders. But Wu Ti's desire for Chinese expansion wasn't to be thwarted as he took China's influence into central Asia. Sixty thousand men were sent two thousand miles across central Asia to enforce the Imperial Will. Although Wu Ti's expansive urge gave new dimensions and influence to the Chinese state it has been estimated that between 129 and 90 BC China lost a quarter of a million of its fighting men, striving to fulfil his ambitions. This expansion, costly in terms of human life, had important consequences for both the east and the west's trade as well as the exchange of ideologies. For centuries this route through central Asia had become a national line of communication and exchange. Countless bales of Chinese silk, the Ceres cloth so highly prized in the Roman world, travelled along this path. In return, swift Sogdian horses and Roman gold went the other way. There was also the steady spread of Persian and Indian influence, but above all, Buddhist religious belief began to spread. However, like the Ch'in dynasty before it, the Han dynasty after Wu Ti's death (87 BC), saw an increasing military struggle for control, which would continue into the third century AD, eventually leading to the 'age of the three kingdoms', one of the bloodiest periods in Chinese history. However, part of the contradiction of this period of history was that there were also significant technological advances that were enhancing the quality of life, such as: a non-magnetic directional compass operated by differential gears, chain pumps for the irrigation of gardens and an ingenious hydraulic powered mechanical puppet theatre. These were extraordinary feats for the time.

The Continued Rise of Buddhism

Alongside the many conflicts, migration continued which shaped and influenced the religious tensions that existed at the time. However, spiritual values continued to thrive. By the second century AD, Buddhism was rising up in the story of China, influencing its beliefs, culture and ideas. Daoism also continued its evolution as the baton was passed on through great philosophical works such as: Liezi – a series of Daoist works which taught that life and death are part of the natural cycle and therefore clinging to one or the other was futile. These teachings also encourage selfless actions and an adherence to the Tao (The Way) in order that the best of endeavour and destiny may meet. There were other philosophers during this period like Wang Chang (27 AD - 97 AD) who continued to focus the mind on higher ideals. His philosophical contribution seems to amalgamate many strands, echoing the naturalistic leaning of the Daoists, whilst borrowing ideals from the Yin-Yang cosmologists of the Han dynasty. For him, natural events had natural causes. Fate was not the result of morality and human behaviour; instead

37

fortune and misfortune were simply the result of fate. He was a naturalist believing that the wonders and anomalies in the world, history and legend all had a natural explanation. His 'critical scientific spirit' did not get much recognition at the time although his work did help purge the masses of China of the 'virus of superstition' that hung over Chinese culture and minds. It is really only since the twentieth century that his unique contribution as an independent thinker has been more fully acknowledged. He is now seen to be one of the forerunners of sceptical reasoning, based on observation and evaluation of the evidence, which resonates much more with western scientific methods of scrutiny.

After the Han dynasty, during the fourth and fifth centuries, a succession of barbarian invasions took place in the north of China. The small kingdoms created then remained until the arrival of the Sui and Tang dynasties in the sixth and seventh centuries AD. These barbarian invasions led to many Chinese fleeing to central and southern China. As a result, new social customs emerged, tea-drinking for instance. Shifts in agriculture and farming took place, such as growing rice instead of millet. Various short-lived dynasties emerged in the south too, which not only competed against one another but with their northern neighbours as well. This period was one of political fragmentation as well as a time of change; many would argue it was also a time of constructive growth because of what would follow in terms of the Buddhist revolution....

The spread of Mahayana (Great Vehicle) Buddhism, with its emphasis on faith, participation, mutual help and a spirit of good will had wide appeal. It was this form of Buddhism that travelled along the central Asian trade routes into China and

Japan. During the third to the sixth centuries, at the time of the barbarian invasions, Buddhism spread rapidly, largely due to the nomads in the northern kingdoms of China. Over time, Indian missionaries such as the monks Dharmaraksa and Kumarajiva travelled to China to explain the faith and to translate the scriptures. This was not a one-way street as Chinese pilgrims travelled along the perilous 'old silk road' to study Buddhism at its source (India). The work of these missionaries changed China's religious outlook. During the centuries of political disunity and social fragmentation there had been a widespread decline of Confucianism except amongst the educated classes. Buddhism provided an antidote to the social ailments of the time. By the sixth century, when the Sui dynasty reunited the country, Buddhism's rise to fame had spread amongst all classes of people.

India's Golden Age?

To complete this summary of the eastern story which was taking place between 500 BC – 500 AD, we need to return to what was unfolding in India post Ashoka Maurya. During Ashoka's reign Buddhism prospered and reached Sri Lanka, where it has flourished ever since

The Mauryan Empire did not survive long after Ashoka's death and in 187 BC. Pushyamitra Shunga overthrew the Mauyrans and the more modest Shunga Empire was established in its place. The Shunga Empire was Hindu in its religion and revivalist in spirit. During this pre-Christian era there was also, alongside the Shunga's, a Greek influence (a legacy from the time of Alexander the Great). Trade and some ideological connections had remained long after he left and this was also part of the shaping of consciousness in India. Menander (Milinda) was one of the few Greeks who left a lasting impression. This was not due to his considerable conquests but in fact, to his alliance to Buddhism. His legend spread all over Buddhist Asia, some of his importance and relevance is chronicled in early Buddhist literature e.g. 'The Questions of Milinda' (a dialogue with a Buddhist monk). So for a while the Indo-Greek kingdoms that were located in the Punjab uneasily co-existed with the Shungas who were in the east and with some central Asian tribes in the northwest. There are contradictory accounts of this period of Indian history, right through to the first century AD, which are scrappily chronicled leaving us unsure about all the various invasions and shifts in power.

Some time in the first or second century AD, Kainishka, king of the Kushans, established an empire, which straddled the mountain passes of the north-west and extended well into the heart of north India. These were people of a central Asian origin. The Kushan kings took their titles from people they had conquered or with whom they had had contact: e.g. King of Kings (Persian), Caesar (Roman), Maharaja (Indian). They were similarly eclectic in religious matters. It was thanks, in part, to their patronage and protection that Buddhism found a foothold in central Asia and then spread to China. It was during this period that two great religious movements gradually cast their shadows across the eastern landscape. There was the Mahayana (Great Vehicle) form of Buddhism, with its worship of Buddha and its emphasis on the lay-person being able to achieve the highest goal. This form of Buddhism had greater appeal than the more austere, monkish religion of the old schools, called Hinayana (Little Vehicle).

Over time Mahayana Buddhism prevailed in Tibet, China, Japan and several of the countries in Southeast Asia. The Hinayana remained strongest in Ceylon and Burma.

The other religious development of great significance during this period was the Bhakti cult, a popular movement setting the loving adoration of God and His grace at the centre of the wheel of life. This spiritual tradition emerged from the Vedas and Upanishads and has been immortalised in the Bhagavad Gita which is probably the most widely read of the eastern religious classics. The Bhakti ideology still sits at the heart of modern-day Hinduism and its 'loving principle' runs through most spiritual teachings.

This Kushan period was followed by the Guptas. By 320 AD the barbarian kingdoms of the west were reduced in number or Indianised and the Gupta Empire emerged. Most of north India and some of the south were included in this expanding empire. For many, this is known as a golden age in India's rich history. By the time of Chandra Gupta II, the Saka invaders in the west of India were also ousted.

Chandra Gupta II's reign (375 AD - 414 AD) was perhaps the most brilliant ancient India was to see. An account left by a Chinese monk, Fa-hsien, who visited India at this time, described it as a very organised state, a classical civilisation, enjoying more peace, prosperity and security than it had done for many centuries. The government was more gentle and virtuous. Poetry, literature and drama flourished. The Sanskrit language was once again widely employed. Gupta architecture set a standard of beauty, simplicity and restraint that many would say has never been repeated. Although they were adherents of Hinduism, they embraced Buddhism, allowing it to co-exist with Hinduism without conflict. This was truly a pluralist society.

If the Chinese were the masters of ceramics, then the Indians of the Gupta age were the masters of metal. They produced staggering iron works five hundred years before the Chinese and one and a half thousand years before the Industrial Revolution! The Gupta period was a time of great scientific development. Their scientists were the first proponents of the concept of zero, which, as I discussed in "Science ...the New God?" was pivotal to the evolution of mathematics, the language on which science depends. In fact all our technological advancements have been built on the back of mathematics. Furthermore, it is becoming clear that everything in the world around us respects and adheres to mathematical equations and formulae. Mathematics is a magician whose tricks are only now beginning to be fully unveiled so we owe a great debt to the Gupta age.

It was also in 500 AD that a Gupta astronomer (Aryabhata) posited that the earth went around the sun (long before Copernicus and Kepler). He also came up with the concept of pi. Amongst his mind-boggling contributions was that he was the first to work out that the circumference of the earth was 24,900 miles! (We now, with all our technological equipment, know it to be 24,873.6 miles…. staggering). Unlike the religious and political turbulence caused by Galileo's discoveries in 1609, which set science against religion, India's own philosophy and ideologies were at complete ease with the idea of an infinite universe. This was entirely compatible with their spiritual traditions and so these scientific discoveries and advancements were embraced rather than feared. All this was happening at the time that the barbarian invasions were taking place in the West as the Roman Empire was being overthrown. The Gupta civilisation went on to shape and dominate the north of India well into the Middle Ages.

I hope the dates, names and places documented here have not distracted too much from the more important story being told, the story of spiritual values triumphing even in the face of the ever-changing landscape of the East. This account of history doesn't seek to glorify what took place in this part of the world, it merely attempts to give it greater credence and relevance. The eastern account of history has many flaws of its own which I've made some attempt to demonstrate and yet a spiritual code keeps trying to express itself, in spite of the countless changes and various hypocrisies. I believe this tenacious 'spiritual code' has eternal relevance and needs to be resurrected now if we humans are not to launch ourselves further into oblivion.

Hopefully, the timeless messages echoed through the great civilizations of the past will find their way into your heart and mind.... I sincerely hope so.

"Everyone should treat all beings as one would want to be treated. True religion is ethical action. To hurt another is to in fact hurt oneself."

Mahatma Gandhi (1869-1948)

CHAPTER 3: THE ISLAMIC INFLUENCE

The Birth of Islam

Prophet Mohammad was a descendant of Prophet Ismail. Muslims consider him the restorer of an uncorrupted original monotheistic faith (Islam). He was restoring a tradition of monotheism, first brought by Abraham, Moses and Jesus, who Muslims also considered to be prophets. They believe that the messages brought by these earlier prophets have been partially changed or corrupted over time but believe the Koran (Qur'an) to be the final, unaltered revelation of God. The word Islam means submission/surrender to God. Mohammed was also active as a social reformer, diplomat, merchant, philosopher, orator, legislator, military leader, humanitarian, philanthropist, and, according to Muslim belief, an agent of divine action.

Prophet Mohammed was born in Mecca in 570 AD. He belonged to the leading tribe of the city, the Quraysh. His own family was respectable but not wealthy. Mohammed the man is largely lost in various eastern interpretations of his role as a prophet; however there are certain stages of his development and role that are broadly agreed upon.

His father, Abdullah, died several weeks before his birth in Yathrib (Medina). His mother died at a place called 'Abwa' when he was six years old. He was raised by his paternal grandfather 'Abd al Muttalib (Shaybah) until the age of eight, and after his grandfather's death by Abu Talib, his paternal uncle. Many years before Mohammad's birth, 'Abd al Muttalib had established himself as an influential leader of the Arab tribe 'Quraysh' in Mecca and took care of the Holy sanctuary 'Kaaba' (the most sacred site in Islam). Mecca was a city-state, well connected to the caravan routes to Syria and Egypt in the north and northwest and Yemen in the south. It was on these caravan routes that Mohammed's early reputation for honesty, reliability and integrity was built. Under the guardianship of his uncle he became a successful businessman and trader.

By the time he was forty he was an affluent, though many would have said unremarkable, market trader. Then in 610 AD, whilst on one of his many retreats to Mount Hira, asleep in a cave, he had a vision of the Archangel Gabriel. This vision left Mohammed with an overwhelming conviction that he had a mission to perform. This compulsion was further cemented by a series of visions and religious experiences throughout his life, which further defined his role as a prophet and his divine purpose. During the first years of his teaching, he spoke of one God, and initially found keen listeners but equally he was mocked by the materialistic and conservative merchants of the city. They found his condemnation of many of the local cults who worshipped or revered trees, wells, stones and over three hundred different idols distasteful, and so they opposed him. His concepts of philanthropy on earth, divine judgment and a life hereafter were also frowned upon at the time.

Over the next twenty years of his life Prophet Mohammed recorded his moments of illumination when he was inspired by divine teachings. He recorded these experiences in short verses, which were gathered after his death to form the Koran. By that time a complete moral code had been formed. The Koran is one of the earliest examples of Arabic literature. The overriding message is of the unity of One God. Mohammed saw God as infinite, merciful and compassionate. The Koran emphasizes the virtue of human charity and inspires a sense of social obligation and duty. The Koran at the time was also attempting to persuade the Jews and Christians to return to the simplicity of the message and the laws Abraham had brought. It is important to note here that Arabs are simply those who lived in Arabia. Their legendary ancestor was Shem and their first prophet was also Abraham. So they are in fact the same Jews referred to in the early books of the Old Testament.

The Prophet was utterly opposed to those consumed by idolatry, immodesty and to heathens (those who had no concept of an afterlife). He spoke passionately and eloquently of heaven and hell, believing the just and devout would taste the sweetness of heaven whilst those who did not embrace the notion of One Supreme God, would become victims of hell. His message as stated earlier, was not well received and for five years he preached in Mecca but only really earned notoriety as there were few adherents. The Quraysh were not enamoured by Mohammed's teachings as they felt he was undermining their hold on Mecca and his concept of there being only one God was also threatening their psychological/spiritual hold on the city. So in 622 AD Mohammed left Mecca because it was clear that his life was increasingly under threat and went two hundred and eighty miles northeast to Medina. Some seventy-five of the first Muslims went with him. This event came to be called Hijra (emigration) and was the turning point in Islam: it is from that year (622 AD) that the Muslim calendar is dated. Mohammed found support in Medina as he built, through dialogue and reason, a multicultural and diverse community where Jews and those of the Islamic faith co-existed peacefully. The first Mosque was founded here by Mohammed and it became a place of refuge, discussion, worship and prayer. It was not exclusively a place of worship for Muslims as he sought to bind the hearts and minds of all the inhabitants of Medina. But as history bears witness, this period is also filled with war and controversy that still divides minds and nations. The story of the conflict between Mecca and Medina is well documented in a number of texts both written by Islamic and non Islamic scholars and for those of you who want to look more closely at the conflict and wars that took place over this period, there is plenty of material to wade through. My mission here is to simply give a flavour of the events taking place at this time rather than become embroiled in the varied accounts that reflect what was happening in this period.

As I've intimated, a number of conflicts took place during this time but the defining encounter took place in 628 AD where Mohammed and his followers surrounded Mecca and eventually an armistice was signed. Mohammed finally re-entered Mecca in triumph in year eight of Hijra (630AD). In the remaining two years of his life he became master of Hejaz (which included Mecca and Medina). This eventual submission by the Quraysh to the Prophet's rule led to the conversion to 'Allah's Law'.

Mohammed died in 632 AD. He left a powerful legacy (far too much to document here). His successors were called Caliphs or deputies of the Prophet of God; they became the heirs to an empire, which swiftly outgrew its origins in Hejaz (in Saudi Arabia, along the borders of the Red Sea). One conquest followed another: Damascus and Syria in 634, Alexandria and the Egyptian Corn lands in 641. As Mohammed had left no sons, disputes amongst his successors went on to dictate Muslim politics for centuries to come. The speedy conquests by Islam both as a faith and a state led to ever-increasing internal divisions. These were complex and many, and are still played out today in the conflicts between the Sunnis (who form the majority of the Muslim world) and the Shiites (the followers of Ali, the fourth Caliph). The Shiite sect was born in the civil wars between the fourth and fifth Caliphs but its conception was also a symptom of the growing unrest among non-Arab Muslims who fought in the armies of Islam but as second-class citizens. This discrimination also fuelled their sense of injustice and discontent. So these ethnic factors are amongst the primary reasons for conflict between Sunnis and Shiites. Added to this were social and economic differences that existed and which maintained the conflict. Those disagreements continue even today.

Muslim armies which later challenged the Byzantine (Roman, largely Christian) and Persian (Iran and the Gulf States)

Empires combined a religious fervour with a military zeal. This has come to be known as 'Jihad' or Holy War. It is however a myth that Muslim armies forced conversion only by the sword. They largely used skilful negotiation and promise of status to maintain their Arab supremacy. As a consequence, within the lands that they conquered, their subjects slowly chose Islam as their faith, eventually leading to the Arabs becoming the minority sector of the Muslim population in those places of occupation. This happened by default rather than by design because as the Muslims used the bureaucratic systems and commercial traditions of the lands they acquired, a natural evolution and blossoming of Islam amongst the people followed. Over time voluntary conversions ended Arab supremacy within Islam.

The Arabs were now thin on the ground in their own kingdoms and so they clung tenaciously to all their special privileges. They managed to do that for a further century. Jews and Christians stood second in their religious and social hierarchy (paying a poll and land tax for privilege and also to avoid military service) as Islam continued to expand. The rapid conquest and expansion during the early 700s would never again be matched in later Islamic history.

The Islamic march in 710 AD went west and conquered the African coast up to Morocco. Visigoth Spain was overrun by 713 in a three year long campaign. It took seven centuries for the Christians of Spain to recover the territories they had lost. In the east the armies of Islam penetrated the Indus Valley and Sind in 712; two years later they were in Kashgar on the fringes of the Chinese Empire. There the expansion stopped, in fact within a century of the Prophet's death, this vast Islamic Empire slowly began to contract. A defining moment in these events and undoubtedly a turning point was the failure of the Arabs to take Constantinople (now Istanbul) by sea in the siege of 717-18. It would be seven centuries before a Muslim conqueror (Mehmet II) would set foot in Constantinople. The Chinese also drove the Arabs back to Ferghana (Turkestan) in 715. The tide of Islamic conquest was turning. Where the Muslims had invaded they largely absorbed the machinery of government and the culture of the occupied territories. This is certainly true of the arts and architecture. For example, in Damascus the Umayyads (Sunni Muslims), having invaded and secured the city, adopted the existing Greco-Roman and oriental traditions. The earliest important Islamic monument is the 'Dome of the Rock' Mosque in Jerusalem, which was completed in 691 AD and is said to be built on the site of Abraham's sacrifice and that of the Prophet's ascension. In 706 the Umayyads also converted the fourth century Basilica of St. John the Baptist into one of the first congregational Mosques. This was one of many conversions from churches to mosques. These conversions represented the cultural confidence of Islam at the time over both Judaism and Christianity. It is important to say that Islam tolerated these two religions largely on account of their monotheism and their recognition of prophets.

China's Glory Days

During the rise of Islam the formation of the T'ang dynasty (168-907 AD) in China had taken place and China had entered one of the most glorious eras in its history. Following the overthrowing of the Siu dynasty a string of very capable rulers followed: T'ai Tsung (626-649 AD), Koa Tsung (649-

683 AD) and a remarkable woman, the Empress Wu (625 – 705 AD). She reorganised and systematized the land-holdings of the previous centuries. This opened up new agricultural areas and encouraged economic development. Empress Wu helped to facilitate the shift in the economic centre of the country from the wheat and millet land found in the north of China to the rich rice growing fields of central China. This shift helped to meet the needs of China's growing population and it also brought prosperity for its people and a generous income for the government. Chang-an, the capital, conveniently located at the eastern end of the central Asian trade routes was also strategically placed to act as a focus for the economic and cultural life of the country. It was a glittering metropolis, which attracted travellers from all over the known world. It was a vast walled city which included parks, temples, palaces, cosmopolitan markets and was home to nearly two million people: Chang-an was an advert for what was best about the T'ang dynasty. By the eighth century the T'ang Empire was the largest the world had ever seen as Chinese rule was extended by conquering the Turks and moved southwards into Vietnam and north-east into parts of Korea. The high point of the T'ang opulence and achievement was reached during the reign of Hsüan-tsung (712-756). It was a brilliant age, which produced breathtaking works of art (pottery, sculpture and painting) and for many is seen as the Golden Age of Chinese poetry. The work of Wang Wei (699-760), Tu Fu (712-770), Li Po (701-762), and others emerged as wonderfully elegant and poignant commentaries on the customs and feelings of that age and their works have left a rich cultural heritage that still speaks to us today.

However, the high point reached at this time also marked the beginning of the decline of the T'ang Empire. Like his predecessors, Hsüan-tsung pursued the imperial ideal and sought to extend Chinese influence into central Asia. By the mid century his armies had reached the Hindu Kush. Here in 751 AD the Chinese came up against the Arabs, a very different foe from those they had been used to (the Uighurs and the Turks). In the battle of Talas, Hsüan-tsung's armies were decisively halted and he never recovered his position in central Asia after that defeat. Here we see the coming together of the two major powers of the East at that time: the Chinese and the Arabs (the Muslims). This is one of many such clashes with which history is littered.

Although the T'ang empire continued until 907, the years that followed Hsüan- tsung were never quite as rich, although beautiful art, pottery and poetry continued to dazzle. Growing financial and economic difficulties led to widespread unrest to such an extent that the fabulous wealth of the Buddhist monasteries was coveted by the hard-pressed government. Between 841 and 845 violent persecutions occurred and thousands of monasteries were dispossessed. Buddhism by this time had flourished and its simple philosophy had evolved into a number of complex philosophical sects. It had comfortably evolved under the shade of the T'ang Empire having spread to Japan and Korea. But it too fell foul of the arrogance and stench of conflict and power. Over the next fifty years, China once again endured an era of division and political collapse. Five separate dynasties emerged and ten independent kingdoms were set up and once again barbarians invaded the north.

East versus West

The rich tapestry of rise and fall of kingdoms, dynasties and empires continued throughout the medieval and renaissance period of history and for the East as well as for the West, religion and spirituality were the uncomfortable companions of war, division and conflict. They co-existed in what many might even describe as an unholy alliance. After all, can war and spirituality ever be on the same side? And yet throughout history there are those who've made their spirituality the basis of war. This is a contradiction that exists both in the East and the West. However, there is a fundamental difference in how this contradiction plays out within these two hemispheres. The primary difference is that in the East, despite the rampant expansion of the aforementioned religions and dynasties, the idea of God or a Divine Designer or some notion of an Imperial influence was never deposed by the evolution of knowledge and the emergence of science. Whereas in the West, science had begun to question the notion of a Supreme deity and that deposition continues today. Many would say that has been to our detriment.

This was not because the eastern world did not see the 'magic' or the potential that the understanding of science was offering. It was simply inconceivable to the eastern cultures that there wasn't a great architect at work. In other words, understanding 'it' (God/life) or its 'workings' did not somehow elevate us beyond 'it', whatever that Supreme presence/influence may be. If we look at this period we can see that the Arab translations from Greek and Syriac (of the classical Greek and Roman texts) pertaining to geography, natural history and the sciences gave the Muslim world a significant lead over Europe in scientific knowledge (what might best be defined as the medieval sciences). This advantage, which was visible in every walk of life, including literature, mathematics, astronomy and architecture, wasn't lost until the fifteenth century! There are a number of factors that handed the West the advantage. Subject to which account of history you gravitate towards, superstition, autocratic leadership, ignorance, arrogance and religious dogma could all be said to have been responsible for the Muslims losing their advantage. For those of you who are really interested in this period of history let your own investigations and judgment be your guide. It's also not unreasonable to suggest that the eastern propensity, despite its obvious 'scientific' interest and heritage, has almost always leaned more towards 'looking inwards' rather than outwards for the answers. This remains true even today – although change is clearly afoot. Whether this change is a good thing or a bad thing is yet to be fully unveiled – the Islamic world is again finding a position of pre-eminence at the table of science and both China and India are moving towards being the superpowers they once were.

I think I should make it clear that my advocating an 'inward-looking habit' doesn't represent an eastern allegiance; my allegiance is to what I perceive to be true. The more you research these matters the clearer I think it becomes; that is that the self and the world are best understood through a merger of the inner and outer universes. Understanding one to the exclusion of the other provides a breeding ground for ignorance, speculation, arrogance and assumption. Therefore, I believe, the imbalances we see evolving in the West are due, in part to the loss of this spiritual and inward-looking focus. Ironically, I also believe this to be true to a lesser extent for the East. So many religious and territorial disputes and conflicts that took place in the East have happened as a result of it losing sight of its own values and principles in pursuit of power. Whatever view you take of history, it seems to me that ego has a lot to answer for, as so many battles have been fought and continue to be fought in its name!

The powerful Islamic rise and influence continued its journey of expansion into Mesopotamia, Persia, Egypt and even into Spain, over several centuries. In many of these instances the Islamic influence is still clearly visible today but the greatest evidence of Islam can now be found in India. Over half of all Muslims still live in India today but the coming together of these two differing forces tells a tale that is arguably the most dramatic in human history.

India Meets Islam

Although some Muslim traders had settled in southern India at the end of the middle ages, the effect of Islam was only really felt in the north with a number of invasions and eventual settlements that took place. It began in Multan (which is now in Pakistan). The key figure in the telling of this story is the highly contentious individual, Mahmud Ghazni. To Muslims he was, and to some still is, an emblematic figure of Islam; a protector of the faith, a great ruler and builder of empires. To Hindus he was and is an oppressor and a fanatic who plundered the riches of India. It was from Multan (which at the time was Hindu) that he began his raids and pillaging. Mahmud at the time was head of a great Muslim empire in Afghanistan (in the eleventh century) and he saw India as a wealthy nest from which he could take and fill his own coffers. This was an age of violence and as we've seen so many times as this historical summary unfolds, it was also a time where there was the meeting of minds. The facilitators of this meeting of minds were the great Sufi Saints who were the first to try and bring Hindus and Muslims together (a point I return to later).

During this period of contradiction and conflict, Mahmud led a dozen expeditions into India in pursuit of its wealth and riches. The most famous of these invasions took place in January 1026 – when he raided the great Hindu temple of Somnath. He tried to justify this raid on the basis of religious grounds, by describing the Hindus as infidels (a premise which had become the basis of so many 'holy wars' or 'Jihad' since the time of the Prophet). The Afghans and Turks of Baghdad may have accepted his justification as 'the defender of the faith' but there are many who still say he simply wanted the riches of Somnath. He set out in November 1025 from Multan and travelled seven hundred and fifty arduous miles south through the desert down to the Arabian Sea, such was his appetite and determination. When he arrived, he ransacked the city, plundered the temple's gold and silver and left it in ruins. His twelve plundering expeditions led to great hatred between the Hindus and Muslims for many years; in some cases this deep-seated resentment remains even today. Mahmud Ghazni's raids were not the last to impact on India's psyche. In 1192 the military advances of the Afghans and Turks into Delhi brought another phase of domination by Muslims. They became the Sultans of Delhi and they established Muslim rule in India. This is where the first actual mosque in India was established and twenty-seven Hindu temples were destroyed in order to build it! This was as much a political statement as a religious one. From the time of Mohammed in the seventh century, Islam's gradual march outwards from the Middle East had led to much invasion and substantial domination. However, it was the Delhi Sultans who realised India couldn't be converted by force - it was too large and diverse and co-existence in some form or fashion was needed. Co-existence had its price though, as Hindus had to pay a head tax to practise their faith. It was the Sufis that would change the religious and spiritual landscape (for a while at least). They brought Islam's mystical tradition to the forefront and spoke of the sanctity of all life. So despite the discrimination against the Hindus in the Middle Ages, wars and pillaging in the north and forced conversions, the Sufis came and laid a foundation for peace.

Once again we see out of the hypocrisy and tragedy of human conflict that kindness tolerance and peace keep trying to make their way to the surface. The next chapter in this story begins with the 'promise of peace' that the Sufi Saints brought to India with the hope that the perpetual conflicts would end and again lead to an Empire of the Spirit rather than an Empire of the Sword. And for a time that endeavour would be fulfilled. There is an incredible contribution from a woman who courageously helped to orchestrate change in what was a very male dominated world, making her contribution all the more exceptional.

Sufism – The Promise of Peace

At the end of the first century of Islam, the Islamic world was beginning one of the most explosive moments in human intellectual history. While theologians and philosophers were busy applying rationalist perspectives to the central issues of human existence and were busy interpreting the Koran, groups of ascetics began to appear, challenging the emergent Imperial culture. They brought a message of integration and peace. They were the Sufis. The key figure credited with the emergence of this beautiful synthesis is Rabi'a al- Adawiyya. Rabi'a was a woman, which makes her contribution all the more incredible in an era of male domination. She was born to a poor family in Basra (Iraq) in 717 AD and was sold into slavery as a girl. As the story goes, she was eventually released by her owner when he saw her continuously performing all night vigils after a full day's work. She led a life of intense religious activity and intellectual conversation. Her role in the development of Sufi thought is illustrated in numerous anecdotes concerning her relationship with Hasan of Basra (who many would say is the founder of Sufism). Hasan was the most famous religious authority of his time, an expert on hadith (traditions of the prophet). He was also acquainted with many of the prophet's companions. He was one of the first advocates of ascetic piety (abstaining from worldly pleasures and steeping oneself in true devotion to God) in Islam and at the same time he was one of the first critical investigators into the issue of divine pre-determination and human free will. So for many not only is he the founder of Sufism but also of Islamic scholastic theology (Kalam).

If, as the anecdotes suggest, Rabi'a knew Hasan, he must have been very old at the time and she very young. What makes Rabi'a quite unique is she is alleged to have competed verbally with Hasan in the tradition of 'spiritual jousting' which was a feature of Sufism. She is said to have demonstrated in these interactions that she was the wiser of the two. Later she went on to synthesize ascetic piety with theological concerns (something the great Hasan never did as he saw them as separate and distinct subjects) which created a new way of thinking and became the very foundation of Sufism. This synthesis combined the Koranic doctrine of the unity of God (tawhid) with ascetic impulses and a continuing investigation of the issue of human free will and divine predetermination. For her, Divine unity could only be achieved by turning one's entire life and consciousness towards God, to consider anything else was a form of idolatry. She went on to constantly criticise Hasan and other spiritual leaders for becoming attached to their ascetic piety and treating it as an end in itself. She felt that those who claimed to despise the world for the sake of God were not paying enough attention to the affirmation of God because if they were they'd have no time to despise the world! It is this infatuation with the Divine (God), a spiritual absorption, that led to her celebrated notion of sincerity (Sidq), or sincere love. For Rabi'a, sincerity was not compatible with acting out of hope for reward or fear of punishment. Here we see another significant point of difference with Hasan of Basra. He was famous for his intensification of the fear of hell in meditation as a way of monitoring and overcoming one's appetite for the carnal self and materialism. Rabi'a rejected the entire notion of reward and punishment and in numerous prayers she is quoted as asking the Deity to deny her paradise if she worshipped out of hope for that, and to condemn her to hell if she only worshipped out of fear. For her, only pure love for God was an antidote to our ills: a principle you may remember, described as Bhakti (love and devotion) in Hinduism. This was said to be one of the three ways to sit in God's heart.

Rabi'a's notion of pure love was welded to complete faith. For her, not to completely trust in God (tawakkul) was a contradiction of the highest order for one who was lost in God's love. She refused to ask for anything of the Supreme Deity as He already knew her condition and needs and would therefore respond accordingly. Such requests would violate both faith and acceptance. She believed this was how one could shed the 'skin of the ego' (which is a central principle of Sufi thought: mystical union). This was not a fatalistic way of living or a passive existence, on the contrary, this absolute acceptance was described by Rabi'a as the key to 'authentic action'. Rabi'a's contribution cannot be overstated. This self-educated, former slave girl of Basra went on to lay a beautiful foundation that would shape Sufism right up to the present time as she and other Sufi Saints helped in the uneasy marriage between India and Islam (Hindus and Muslims). Some of the other Sufi Saints that built Sufism into a gentle and beautiful chorus of peace include: Junayd (910 AD), Bistomi (875AD), Tustari (896AD), Hallaj (922AD) and Quashayri (986-1074AD). To them much is owed. Unfortunately as wonderful as the Sufi contribution was, it remained insufficient to address all the differences between Islam and the natives of India who felt stripped of their riches, ideology and culture.

"A person's true wealth is the good he or she does in the world."

Mohammed (570 – 632)

CHAPTER 4: FROM THE MONGOLS TO THE MOGULS

Eastern Evolution or Further Demise?

To the European, Asia was fabulously wealthy, a mysterious amalgam of culture, philosophy and splendour but infinitely dangerous. It was a place where the Saracens (heathens) had deprived Christendom of its rightful centre in Jerusalem. There was at this time (the Middle Ages and Renaissance period) the rise of the destructive and devilishly cruel Mongols who would go on to establish the largest land empire ever and dramatically change the history of the Asian continent. Occasional travellers to the East, men such as Marco Polo (1254-1324), brought back accounts of what they found there. Sadly the small amounts of factual knowledge were embellished with innuendo and imagination, leaving the average educated European totally ignorant of the real condition of the East. With European expansion and subsequent invasions this would eventually change.

In the same way, the East showed very little interest in the West. It was totally absorbed with the spread and intermingling of its own cultures. Islam, and before that Buddhism, were spreading their influence well outside of the incubators in which they'd been conceived. Unlike medieval Christianity, these religions were largely assimilated into their new cultural homes, with benefit to both the religion and the culture to which it had now become attached.

I've not, apart from in my introduction, made any significant references to south east Asia but it's important to say that Japan and Korea eventually found their place as centres of cultural influence alongside their older siblings China and India. South and East Asia's evolution reflects much of what was taking place in the East generally. Both cultures (Korea having formerly been under Japanese rule) are built largely on Buddhist principles and so morality and ethics were and remain pivotal to how these cultures have unfolded. There are of course differences in ideology and religious practices, but the principles of: meditation, karma, rebirth, heaven, The Way (Dao), various Confucian ideals and concepts such as destiny versus free will and society versus individual, have run in an unbroken way through the generations, shaping the psyche of that part of Asia. I will explore this in greater depth later (see Chapter 6).

For now let me return to the Indo-Chinese evolution... or is this evolution really demise? I've partly told the story of the Muslim conquest of India by Turks which began in the twelfth century and continued for a further three hundred years in the north of India. This expansion had absorbed Iran along the way and also had defeated the Byzantine Emperor Romanus in 1071. In 1076 Jerusalem was captured, increasing the Turkish pressure on India. By the thirteenth century, successive rulers pushed, by stages southwest to

Gujarat and east to Bihar and Bengal from Delhi. Then in the fourteenth century, they moved across the challenging Vindhya mountains into southern India. By 1327 the conquest of the Delhi Sultanate was so advanced that Sultan Muhammad bin Tughluq founded a second capital in the Deccan. The new capital in Deccan was called Tughluqabad. This was a majestic city announcing the 'foreign-ness' of the new dynasty's great power and opulence. The city contained a great palace, a massive citadel, battlements encased in the surrounding walls. There were also pointed arches, domes and minarets of mosques, colleges and royal tombs. All these features had travelled from western Asia. This was all alien to India. So was the mixture of Turkish and Persian blood and the language which defined this new ruling class. The Sultan was legitimized by the Caliph, the religious head of the Muslims, with a traditional robe of honour, underlining acceptance of his dominion. This foreign domination echoed across all of north India and the Sultan's influence went on to permeate all aspects of culture, such as: lexicography (vocabulary) and language in all its forms, architecture, poetry, scientific enquiry and history to name a few.

Hinduism's on-going battle with Islam continued during this period as new mosques were built and the Ulema (leaders in communal prayer, expounders of the holy Koran and the sayings of the Prophet) set their new orthodoxy against the old orthodoxy of Hinduism. The Sufi Order of Muslim Mystics was busy preaching personal devotion rather than formal ritual as being the best approach to a relationship with God. As a result of their message, a process of mass conversion to Islam took place in the areas now known as Pakistan and Bangladesh. Another of the many interesting contradictions worth noting is that in the first century of Turkish rule in India all of the rulers were either slaves or descendants of slaves. The use of slaves in high position since the early Turkish dynasties was commonplace. Many of these slaves were educated sons of captured chiefs and had achieved distinction through their ability and loyal service. The irony here is that these former slaves then helped maintain the Muslim minority in power, leaving many Hindus feeling like and in some cases treated like slaves in their own country! So Hindi (India's primary language) was tolerated but Sanskrit was preferred and used more readily in administration and official circles. Alongside it a new language developed, which reflected the cross-fertilisation of culture, beliefs and ideas. That language was Urdu. Urdu was a mixture of Sanskrit, Arabic and Turkish. At first, it was used only by common people but by the seventeenth century it was accepted as a beautiful medium of literary expression.

By way of comparison, let us look at what was happening in China around the same period to see if the East was indeed evolving or in fact contributing to its own demise.....

The Chinese Experience

The period of political disunity that emerged after the fall of the T'ang dynasty was brought to an end in 960 by the Sung emperors, who ruled from 960 to 1297. They established the third great Chinese dynasty. Their three hundred year reign was not as confident, expansionist and aggressive as that of the Han and T'ang dynasties and as a result of some unwise alliances and various conflicts their rule was arguably not as potent and grand. However, the Sung periods saw significant advances in the fields of medicine, biology and mathematics, as well as military techniques. The growing technical knowledge of this era helped with water irrigation and conservancy measures, which improved the food supply for the growing population. Maritime commerce also began to flourish as new trade routes across the seas began to emerge as an alternative to land routes and whole new areas of trade were also being exploited. Improved navigation methods and the construction of larger more seaworthy ships aided this development. Initially a lot of this trade was under Arab and Persian control as there were sizeable foreign communities to be found at various posts along the China coast. However, under the Sung dynasty that began to change and the influence and power passed to Chinese merchants who rapidly came to dominate the trade in precious silks, porcelains and fine Chinese handicrafts, which were in demand especially in south-east Asia. The Chinese economy, despite the on-going political difficulties, expanded under the Sung emperors. This was a period of rich technical medieval science and cultural achievement. The Sung genius was also reflected in painting, which particularly focused on impressionistic landscape and nature paintings. Due to a decline in Buddhism, religious themes were less in favour. Literature, which had broken new ground in the T'ang dynasty, prospered even more at this time and new forms of literature emerged as a result. There was a rapid increase in schools and academies. The intellectual renaissance of the Sung period is largely explained by the advances in printing and book production, which helped to generate a high level of literacy amongst its people. Printing led to great advances in scholarship. Vast compilations of classics, early historical records and encyclopaedias began to emerge. Although this activity began with the T'ang dynasty it really took off in the Sung period and has been maintained ever since. In fact, the Chinese are the most assiduous compilers of documents in the world. This literary revolution helped the revival of Confucianism at a time when Buddhism began to lose its dominant grip in China and as scholars and philosophers began to reinterpret the early Chinese philosophical and political ideals. The work of Chu Hsi (1130-1200) was significant in this shift in consciousness and its impact was such that it dominated the Chinese outlook until the nineteenth century.

From the Mongols to the Moguls

As stated earlier, Europe's idea of the East was distorted but from time to time during the middle ages Europeans were reminded of how small their corner of the world really was. Rumours would come out of the East, of a land, which stretched to the very edge of the earth. A land inhabited by restless clans of herdsmen who lived on their horses and shifted their black hide tents hundreds of miles in their annual quest for new pastures. The men were described as squat and slit-eyed, they were said to have no noses. They worshipped the wind and lived in the wilderness. They were the Mongols, arguably the most devastating wave of conquerors to emerge from central Asia. They established an empire twice the size as that of Alexander the Great and four times that of the Roman Empire. Their kingdom stretched across Europe and Asia, from Germany in the west to Japan in the east. Their might and influence was felt in the north-east on the emerging Russian state. In China Kublai Khan (grandson of Genghis Khan) brought an end to the Sung dynasty. In the Middle East the empire of Hulagu Khan (c.1216-1265) transformed the Muslim world. This began with Genghis Khan's invasion of Transoxiana in 1219 and was completed by Hulagu Khan's plundering and capturing of Baghdad in 1258. The Mongols' part in history is an unusual one, as on one hand their crusades and advances were brutal and unforgiving, whilst on the other hand they came to the rescue of Byzantium twice, by all but destroying their Turkish enemies in 1243 in Antolia and in 1402 by triumphantly carrying Bayezid, the Ottoman Sultan, off the battlefield at Ankara. Also it should be said for purposes of balance that for western Christians the Mongols gave the hope of a potential ally to break the Muslim encirclement of Jerusalem. In fact, there has been a long held western belief that the Mongols were led by Prester John, the legendary Christian King of some distant eastern country. This has never been verified and has become the stuff of legend as it is the Mongols Gengis Khan and his grandson Kublai Khan that are remembered most for their conquests and rulership. Great chronicles have been written about these two world conquerors. After the many conquests listed above, their attention turned to China. In 1213 the Mongols stormed the Great Wall. Within two years Peking fell. By 1222 much of China had been seized. In fact, this was true of Russia too. Genghis Khan did not maintain rulership of such a vast area by military strategy alone: he had codified Mongol clan law in a book called Yasa (this remained the basis of Mongol moral and civil code until the twentieth century). Genghis Khan died in 1227 at the age of 60 but his legacy continued. He left behind a vast kingdom that was well coordinated with efficient communicators and better trade routes between the

East and Europe. This led to a variety of nervous and in many cases fruitless dialogues as the Europeans and Christendom tried to negotiate to see if they could 'tame' the great Mongolian influence. These did not amount to much as the Mongolians sat comfortably in their dominion over their conquests and felt they had the will of God behind them. There is a notable exchange between Pope Innocent IV and Guyuk the Great Khan. When Pope Innocent suggested that the Great Khan be baptized Guyuk said : "How do you know that the words which you speak are with God's sanction? From the rising of the sun to its setting, all lands have been made subject to me. Who can do this against God's will?" He then ordered the Pope to submit to him and concluded ominously: "If you do not observe God's command and if you ignore my command, I shall know you as my enemy. Likewise I shall make you understand. If you do otherwise God knows that I know". This illustrates the confidence, or was it arrogance, of the Mongols. There is much more that could be said about their reign but for the purposes of this work I believe this is sufficient. I am concerned here with the re-defining of history: the reshaping of lands, the evolution of languages and the myriad of cultures that have emerged out of the battle between the 'arrogance of the ego' and the 'humility of the spirit'...It is the battle between these two opposing positions which I think has led to our spiritual demise despite the appearances of modern-day progress.

The Chinese conquest by the Mongols, although started by Genghis Khan, was in fact completed by his grandson in 1279, establishing a new dynasty, the Yuan. This dynasty was brutal in conquest and very centralizing, ready to use Muslims, Christians and others from the Mongol conquests in western Asia to supervise Chinese provincial administration in what had become the Mongolian way. Kublai Khan had been very eclectic in his rule, accepting the moral code and philosophy of Confucius as that was already in operation and working. However, Kublai Khan's chameleon like approach did not last despite the Yuans' attempts to rebuild canals and respect Buddhism as well as the Confucian ideals. This caused irritation amongst some scholars as there were limited official state appointments offered to non-Chinese individuals. These efforts did not prevent the demise of Mongolian rule in China and opened the door to the Ming dynasty in 1368. The Ming dynasty ushered in over two hundred and fifty years of stable and relatively prosperous rule.

What of India and the Mongols?

The attraction and seduction of India continued to exert a pull on those who admired its wealth and mystery. Although in the main it was the physical treasure that drew many invaders, we must not lose sight of the amazing spiritual wealth India has been responsible for offering to the world. The Mongols had tried to invade north India between 1295 and 1306, devastating the countryside around Delhi in the process but the Khalji Sultans (of Afghan descent) not only kept the Mongols at bay but caused them to retreat. India didn't have to deal with Genghis Khan but they had another equally devastating threat of their own; his name was Timur (which means Iran). He became known as Tamerlane. This name was derived from an injury in battle that left him with a limp. He became known as Timur-i- Lang, Timur the Lame or Tamerlane.

Born in 1336 in Transoxiana, he was a Muslim and regarded his conquests as something of a holy war (Jihad), to remind other Muslims (such as the Ottomans) of their duties to Islam. Tamerlane was more ruthless and reckless than Genghis. He built his power base on the remnants of the empire of Genghis Khan. His evolution to power began in a similar way to Genghis', gathering together small nomadic tribes and slowly building an empire from there. Then in quick succession he conquered Transoxiana (Uzbekistan, Tajikistan and southwest Kazakhstan), Persia, Syria, Turkistan and most of Asia Minor. In 1398 he proclaimed a holy war against the Infidels, and like many before him, attracted by the wealth of India, descended on her like a vulture securing its prey. Tamerlane was ruthless and at the siege of the fort of Kator, ten thousand Hindus were killed in an hour! His horrendous signature was left on India in this year long siege as he had all the skulls of the dead heaped into a pile in the shape of a minaret, presumably a symbolic justification of his 'holy war'. He went on to ransack and capture Delhi in a famous battle with the Sultan Mahmud on the field of Pam'pat. Over a million Hindus were massacred. Many thousands were then carried off into slavery and subjected to terrible cruelty. The menace of Tamerlane and his many military acquisitions continued until 1405 when he died. The huge state he created then collapsed. In Persia those who had followed him (Timurids) held on for a further century (1502), however, in India his descendants ruled as great Moguls from 1526 – 1857.

The Transfer of Power

The Moguls originated from central Asia having come down the same corridor of history as Alexander the Great, Genghis Khan and Tamerlane through the Khyber Pass in late 1525. They attacked from Kabul and at the fifth time of trying they breached India's borders and her resistance in another battle played out in Pam'pat. History was clearly repeating itself. The difference here though was that this battle was between a Muslim invader (Barbur) and Muslim incumbent (Ibrahim). This battle unlike previous ones in this part of the world, eventually led to a much needed peace and a growing religious tolerance. Barbur entered Delhi peacefully and did not repeat the actions of Mahmud Ghazni, who had pillaged the Somnath Temple several centuries earlier. In fact, the Moguls now brought a quiet respect for India and devotion to Sufism that would influence their three hundred and thirty year reign.

It was the grandson of Barbur (Akbar) who was to become one of India's greatest kings. It was he who would change the relationship between Muslims and Hindus. He was only thirteen when he came to the throne in 1556 and although he remained illiterate the whole of his life, he demonstrated unexpected skills in rulership. Over the next ten years he expanded the Mogul empire in the shadow of the ever-diminishing Mongol empire. He became interested in India's diverse religions and philosophies. It is in this exploration and examination of philosophy and spirituality that his uniqueness as a ruler is best demonstrated. He was a very different kind of sovereign.

It was Akbar who lifted the much-hated head-tax on Hindus

and encouraged religious tolerance by embracing all of India's religions. Once again we see history repeating itself; Akbar's approach has many similarities to Asoka's reign (273-232BC). He too wanted to see a return to the 'empire of the spirit' not of the sword. During this era there was one clear example of this beautiful ideal…Sikhism.

Sikhism – Another Attempt at Peace

In the sixteenth century the Sikh religion emerged out of the ongoing tension between Hinduism and Islam. Their first Guru, Nanak (1469-1539) said: "There is no Hindu or Muslim, we are one and there is only one God". He stressed the need for charity; he didn't believe that renunciation, performance of rites, ceremonies and acts of austerity would lead to enlightenment. For him it was good deeds that paved the way. It is no surprise that the new faith he fostered, called Sikhism, was influenced by the teaching of Islam, Hinduism, Sufism and the Bhakti saints. The age in which Nanak lived was characterised by political chaos and religious oppression and this influenced his exploration and enquiry. He travelled widely in order to question, challenge and listen to the different philosophical arguments put forward by these faiths. And he reasoned his way to a philosophy that disregarded rituals, rites and inequality. He did embrace some of Islam, Hinduism, Sufism and Bhakti principles where they were congruent with his unwavering Monotheism. He considered poetry, art, music and philosophy to be important but religion was considered the highest endeavour for attaining spiritual wisdom and knowledge of the eternal truth. Hence his emphasis on charity, worship, hard work and ethical conduct.

Nanak's philosophical ideas are crystallised in numerous songs, hymns and oral discourses which were collectively called the Gurbani, literally meaning the 'Guru's word'. However, the Japji Sahib and Asa Di Var are his most important contributions to Sikhism. They outline the ideas and themes central to Nanak's spiritual and philosophical thought. These are expressed largely through devotional hymns and poetic compositions. The influence of Japji and Asi Di Var continued long after his death. The fifth guru of Sikhism, Arjan Dev, compiled Nanak's poetry in the Adi Granth, which, after the tenth guru (Gobind Singh), came to be known as Guru Granth Sahib. Nanak was passionate about there being only one God who he described as formless, infinite and immortal – Nirankar. This is why he disapproved of the idol worship found in Hinduism with its many Gods (polytheism). He felt the proof of God was visible in nature and that he was not subject to the laws of reincarnation as he could not die – he was not subject to decay – he was immortal! And by chanting God's name one's sins can be purified. For him there was no ritual in this, this was simply ethical action which is essential if one is to find salvation. He also stressed the need for honesty, kindness and compassion for it is these virtues that will help man attain wisdom and communion with God. It was because of these principles and values that he vehemently condemned the Hindu caste system. He believed in a casteless society and for that to be achieved he believed that the ego had to be conquered. Only when the ego is conquered will all other sins (anger, greed, lust, pride and attachment) fall away and the spirit of brotherhood and equality take their place. These values resonate with the Sufi saints (who represented the mystical side of Islam) and the Bhakti saints (who could be considered to have offered a similar contribution to Hinduism). Nanak managed to carry this message to the common people, therefore reaching a wider audience making his contribution to the eastern world quite unique. His philosophy broke down barriers and encouraged integration, what he was offering was accessible to all. This offered a feeling of worthiness and self-confidence to the masses, which his nine successors up to and including the last Guru, Guru Gobind Singh, emulated.

Nanak's position and the principles of Sikhism appealed to Akbar and it was he who donated the land where the Golden Temple in Amritsar was built and still stands today. Akbar said: "it cannot be wisdom to assert the truth of one faith over another" and this was one of many statements that demonstrated his belief in integration. For him "the wise person makes justice his guide and learns from all faiths, only such a person may find the key to 'all' where it had once been lost". This message seems as relevant now as it was five hundred years ago…maybe even more so! Akbar's focus was on finding common ground between all faiths. To this end he invited scholars, sages, gurus, priests etc. of all faiths (Jains, Christians, Hindus, Muslims, Jews and Parsees) to discuss and compare their faiths so that the 'truth' might be found. Despite the huge differences in India he held weekly satsangs (spiritual gatherings) in order to try and foster religious tolerance. Akbar was doing in the sixteenth century what no one else in the world was doing at that time. In fact, his efforts pre date the 'age of enlightenment' that didn't come along for another two hundred years! It is accurate to say that it was he who brought in the 'age of reason' (at the time when Europe was going through the renaissance period).

Akbar was a true humanitarian, interested in one religion, equality and fairness. He was a visionary; his big ideas would only be pursued in Europe some two hundred years after his death. After a fifty year reign he left a legacy on which the Mogul empire would thrive until the time of the British Empire (in 1857). When he died (1605), India was the wealthiest nation in the world materially, but it could be argued it was also the wealthiest nation spiritually too. Ironically the promise of an extended 'Golden Age' in India was lost - due again to our old friend 'the ego'. It would be the extravagance of the Moguls and their over indulgence in the seventeenth century that would eventually lead to their demise, despite their countless achievements in the arts, architecture, science, technology and literature. India would soon again fall foul of foreign invaders....this time the British.

In this chapter of history we see the devastation brought by the Mongols and the Moguls as they sought to impose their will and change the landscape of the East. We also see the desperate attempts by the Sufis and the Sikhs to turn minds and hearts away from war and towards peace and enlightenment. Sadly the tide of war kept pushing back their charge, as greed, and the pursuit of power maintained its force.

"When the personal life is cultivated, the family will be regulated; when the family is regulated, the state will be in order; and when the state is in order there will be peace throughout the world! All must regard cultivation of their personal life as the root or foundation of peace and order."

Confucius (551-479 B.C.)

CHAPTER 5: ANTIQUITY LOSES ITS GRIP

The Chola Age

In the tenth century, another civilization, the Chola, a Tamil power, dominated and shaped the medieval kingdoms of southern India (900 –1300 AD). The Cholan heritage goes back to the time of the great king Asoka and the Maurya Empire in the third century BC. The Cholas were known as the 'Athenians of India'. The Chola age was a wonderful period of Indian art, worship and tradition (especially Hinduism). In fact, their worship of Shiva continues today maintaining an unbroken tradition right back to 1010. The main figure who established the foundation for this Tamil domination of southern India was 'Rajaraja the Great'. Through him this Tamil empire became one of the world's great powers. The Chola period was one of strange contradictions. On the one hand they used blood and violence to expand their kingdom and yet on the other hand preached justice and virtue. Here again we see the spirituality of the East fighting for its place in a world that was losing its way. Even today, Southern India, in large part due to this influence, still holds onto much of the abundance and virtue conceived at this time. This region certainly has a greater continuity of thriving Indian traditions, as it has been less affected by the numerous invasions that impacted on the north and so has retained much more of its cultural integrity. The Cholas left a lasting legacy. Their patronage of Tamil literature and their zeal in building temples has resulted in some great written works and stunning architecture.

The Chola kings were avid builders and envisioned the temples in their kingdoms not only as places of worship but also as centres of economic activity. They pioneered a new form of government and established a disciplined bureaucracy. Rajaraja was pivotal in this as he perfected the administrative organisation by creating a strong and centralised machinery and by appointing local government authorities. He installed a system of audit and control by which the village assemblies and other public bodies were held to account while not curtailing their autonomy.

From the 23rd to the 29th year of Rajaraja's rule his dominions enjoyed peace and the king devoted his energies to the task of internal administration and creating religious tolerance. He also, during this time built the famous Rajarajesvara temple in Thanjavur. Although Rajaraja was an ardent follower of Saivism (one of the 4 major streams of Hinduism) he was nevertheless tolerant towards other faiths and creeds. He also had several temples for Vishnu constructed and he encouraged the construction of the Buddhist Chudamani Vihara at the request of the Srivijaya king Sri Maravijayatungavarman.

The Chola dynasty was eventually overthrown by the

Pandyan dynasty, another great Tamil power. The Pandyan's heritage, goes back to five or six centuries BC. The two great Tamil dynasties waged many wars over many centuries, each one leading to the rise and fall of the other. Power and dominion changed hands between them many times. During the thirteenth century, Marco Polo described the Pandyan dynasty as the richest empire in existence as its physical wealth, resources and beauty were unrivalled anywhere else on earth.

The Ming Dynasty

By 1382 the Mongols had been expelled from China by the founder of the Ming Dynasty, Hung-Wu. This renewal brought by the Ming Dynasty in China ran, in many ways, parallel to what was happening in India. Like so many times in history, we see that invasion, migration of people and ideology keeps re-writing the script of a country/continent and changing the socio-religious-political landscape in the process. A great deal happened during the Ming years, but it could be summarized in two phrases: 'physical reconstruction' and 'institutional renewal'. China saw the building of bridges, refurbishment of irrigation works, enlarging of canals and paving of highways. All of which expanded production and trading. There was growth in the cultivation of cotton, maize, sweet potatoes, peanuts, tea, etc. And also the large scale production of porcelain. The demand for cotton cloth and silk also grew rapidly. Institutional renewal matched the changes in infrastructure and social opportunity, as a new code of administration and criminal law, overturning the Mongol influence, was established in 1397 and by 1511 the dynasty had compiled a collection of statutes setting out imperial rule and purpose. Although Hung-Wu had been a Buddhist monk, he restored Confucianism as the guiding principle for the state and its emperors. So once again the changing of the guard, between Buddhism and Confucianism, continued to play itself out in the hearts and the minds of the Chinese. This return to Confucian ideals brought with it meritocracy. This was not a system based on hereditary and feudal aristocracy. Those who wished to enter state service had to study the ancient Confucian classics and take examinations in order to achieve their positions within the hierarchical structure. These exams insured impartiality and uniformity. They also ensured that the genuinely talented and hard working could and would rise to the top. As the Confucian classics were conceived with an emphasis on improving the nature of the individual and the right ordering of society as their foundations, these exams ensured candidates acquired a common attitude of mind, a public spirit and morality. This was important for both the cultural unity and the administrative efficiency of the vast Ming Empire. This system was not without its flaws, but its primary premise of building a society on principle and merit has global value. A boy in sixteenth century China had more chance of rising through the ranks of the civil service on his merits than he would have in twenty-first century Britain!

The economic security and prosperity of this time also brought a flowering of the arts: bronzes, porcelain, enamelled ware, extraordinary lacquer work, painting and calligraphy to name a few. In sixteenth century China, the arts – especially landscape painting - became a spiritual exercise, in which artists sought to tell the story of the inner harmonies and principles of nature. Once again, as has been true from the time of Confucius and of Lao Tzu, man's relationship with nature was for China the ultimate love song and artistry was another way in which this song could be sung.

The demise of the Ming dynasty came in the manner that is so familiar in history. The founder of the Ming dynasty had begun as a leader of peasant revolts against the oppressive demands of the Mongols. He had tried to change the system and had largely been successful but there remained an underbelly of corruption, which eventually brought, along with war, the toppling of this artistic, cultured, expansive era in China. So the Ming dynasty, which had initially been the restorer of native rule and Confucian ideals, eventually fostered such discontent that it was overthrown and replaced by the Manchu. China again fell under the influence and rule of nomads but this time they were a welcome relief from the growing corruption under Ming rulership. This was an uprising where internal forces (Li Tsu-Cheng – a Chinese rebel) sided with the external invader (Nurhachi-a Juchen Chief) and reclaimed China from its paralysis and corruption.

For those more interested in the Indian and Chinese experience there is plenty of literature examining - and in some cases comparing - these two giants of the East. What I've tried to do here is to merely sketch the story of their individuality as well as to highlight some of their obvious similarities.

The next two hundred and fifty years would serve up many more contradictions in the East as the world began to rapidly expand and different influences, perspectives and ideologies began to emerge, especially the influence of science. For those of you interested in science's role, you may want to take a closer look at my other book, 'Science, The New God?' which is the first part of this trilogy.

Asia Meets Europe on Several Fronts

The thought that the withering Mogul empire would one day be replaced by a European one seemed ludicrous at the time especially when the greatest threat in the early and mid seventeenth century came from India's menacing neighbours, Persia and Afghanistan. There was also the formidable Hindu power of the Maharatta Confederacy. In the end as a result of a series of battles that culminated at the Battle of Paniput in 1761, the various pretenders to the throne eliminated each other leaving the door open for the Europeans.

About two decades before the battle of Paniput it was becoming clear that a new relationship was developing between the Islamic political powers and the Europeans who were trading on the subcontinent. There were a number of enclaves: the British were in Madras, Bombay and Calcutta, the French in Pondicherry, the Portuguese in Goa and Diu. However, this friendly co-existence and co-operation began to change as a result of the increasing rivalry between the British and the French. When the English arrived in India, the Dutch and Portuguese were already there, the Germans and the Danes had also begun to show an interest. The Moguls however became friendly with the English and in the seventeenth century the East India Company's ships had even been used as the Mogul Empire's navy. By the beginning of the eighteenth century the French interest seemed to have subsided but in the reorganisation of Colonial enterprises the French East India Company was put on a better footing and because it was becoming a more profitable concern this reignited France's interest and would eventually change the landscape of India again. So with their control of two very important islands in the Indian Ocean – Reunion and Mauritius – the French were well positioned. For the next one hundred years or near enough the tug of war between France and Britain continued as each sought to stake their claim. However, it was the British who steadily found themselves in the ascendancy, slowly increasing their grip on India and its people. There were many terrible wars between the two as they strove to extend their respective European Empires.

There are too many defining moments to mention during this period of ebbing and flowing of power and influence. Suffice it to say that the British did eventually claim dominion over India after many treaties, broken agreements and wars etc., For example the Black Hole of Calcutta (1754), the Seven Years War (1757-1763), the dissolution of the French East Indian Company (1767), Lord North's Regulating Act of 1773, just to name a few.

The Eastern landscape continued to change under the weight of so many competing interests. In China, the Ming Dynasty had been replaced by the Manchu Dynasty, also known as the Ch'ing (pure) Dynasty. They gave China good government, internal peace and increased the empire under the dynamic K'ang Hsi (1662 – 1722) and his successors, Yung Chang (1723 – 35) and the extremely able Ch'ien Lung (1736 – 96). During this period the Chinese empire had the lands adjoining China under proper control, the Mongols were crushed, the area northwest of China was organised under the name Sinkiang ('the new dominion'); the Tibetan Dalai Lama became a Chinese nominee and the borders within Manchuria were stabilised by a treaty with the Russians. In addition Korea, Annam, Burma and Nepal all acknowledged China as their celestial emperor. The remarkable continuity of Chinese history survived despite the numerous invasions and imperial changes - just as is the case for India. The habit of paying respect for the past, for ancestors, for long established customs and practices of the Confucian ethic, continued to stand firm. In the nineteenth century it was this attachment to the past (Chinese conservatism) and reluctance to change that many would say proved to be disastrous in the face of the aggressive, technologically advanced culture of Europe, which had begun to take a grip on the world. This meant China began to fall behind. For the most part it continued to happily 'look back' whilst the western world galloped ahead. The same can be said for China's political history in the nineteenth century, as there is substantial evidence of extortion and injustice by a corrupt civil service that continued until the end of the empire in 1912. So the closed world of China did not welcome the dynamic eruptions and progress, which were taking place in the West. China did not feel threatened by the West's progress as it saw the West as a puny force, overreaching itself as a consequence of its arrogance. Coupled to this, it believed the West's ideology was flawed and doomed to failure. This outlook was to seal the Chinese fate and unquestionably handed the West the initiative on the world stage.

Jesuits in China

There was one significant exception to China's refusal to embrace Western values and way of life. This was their relationship with the Jesuits. A lot of knowledge and principles from 'outside' of Asia have shaped some aspects of Eastern culture and we can see some evidence of that in the T'ang dynasty (AD 618 – 907) when the earliest Christian missionaries went to China. The overwhelming majority of these missionaries were Catholics. The most notable to have entered China since the T'ang dynasty was a Jesuit, Matteo Ricci in 1601. He was an astronomer and mathematician and he started what was to become a tradition: Jesuits acting as scientific advisors to the Chinese. Their general input was appreciated and their input in the reforming of the Chinese calendar was considered invaluable. In 1692 an edict of religious tolerance was issued. The Jesuits were equally adaptable in their attempts to convert the Chinese. Ricci and other Jesuits achieved some success by desisting from arguing about the compatibility of Christianity and Confucian ideals and so religious tolerance and religious persuasion co-existed for a while.

However, in 1715, the Pope condemned some of the Chinese 'rites' and cultural and religious practices, and the previously benevolent K'ang Hsi, who had backed the Jesuits, was deeply offended by this insult to Chinese culture; The Pope's new decrees effectively ended the spread of Chinese Christianity and thus hastened the Papal dissolution of the Jesuits in 1773.

This was a loss to the Chinese too as their contact with the Jesuits had enabled them to acquaint themselves with the inventions of the West. Not that Chinese culture was set up or ready for the changes that the West was about to undergo during the industrial revolution, but that a better understanding of the western mind and the power that was accruing at that time may well have helped, even prevented much of the conflict between East and West in the nineteenth and twentieth centuries. This lack of comprehension was a mutual issue, as the Europeans equally lacked a depth of understanding about the Chinese and the Indians as well as the Middle and Far East. The very insular nature of China helped by its geography of mountains, deserts and seas meant that for millennia China had known only cultural inferiors. And so it is understandable that they saw their state as 'the' state and their culture as 'the' culture. Therefore, their Emperor was the only legitimate ruler below heaven. This position made diplomatic and trade connections and relationships with the Europeans difficult. This was further reinforced by China's self-sufficiency. The Europeans wanted China's silk, porcelain, tea etc; China at the time wanted nothing from Europe. So as the European forces grew, it was against this background that the nineteenth century conflicts took place.

It's worth noting that Japan closed its doors to the West even more firmly. The Europeans arrived in Japan in 1542-43 and taught the Japanese to use firearms and build fortifications. They also brought Christianity, which the Japanese embraced. However, by 1638 Christianity had been uprooted by force as it had come to be identified with political subversion and external aggression. The Japanese then shut their ports to the Europeans and whereas they had previously been a roving people with a reputation as fearless soldiers and pirates, they became introverted and traded less with the world, the only exceptions being China and the Dutch. As the Jesuits had been a conduit for western science to filter into China, the Dutch performed a similar service for the Japanese, bringing news of western science and especially medicine to their shores.

Philosopher Meets Warrior

The great thinkers and philosophers of the East continued their march for truth during the sixteenth and seventeenth centuries. In India there were minds such as: Madhusudana Sarasvati who produced major scriptural works but whose greatest contribution was arguably promoting that the path of Bhakti (the path of love and devotion) was a swifter route than Gyan (the path of knowledge) to Moksha (liberation). Around the same time Dharmaraja Adhvarin, like many of the great philosophers before him, wrestled with epistemology (theory of knowledge). For him there were six distinct means of knowledge: perception, inference, comparison, postulation, verbal testimony and non-apprehension. He discusses these means of knowledge at length in his major work: The Vedanta Parabhasa.

Meanwhile, the fundamental conflicts remained between Hinduism and Islam and by the seventeenth and eighteenth centuries Sikhism was well established, but rather than being a faith that would bridge the differences in India, as first hoped, it was now clearly carving its own path. Islam continued to produce great philosophers too, many influenced by the mystic tradition of the Sufis, such as Mulla Sadra (1574-1641) although he did not accept all aspects of

Sufism. He produced several major works amongst which were: The Four Journeys of the Soul, The Book of Origin and Return, and Descending from the Divine Throne... He also produced commentaries on the Koran and went on to consolidate the School of Isfahan, which his teacher Mir Damad had established. This philosophical school was a turning point in the history of Islamic philosophy in Iran and as a result produced some of the greatest masters of Islamic philosophy. The thrust of Mir Damad's work was that God is the ultimate perfection and 'becoming' is a spiritual journey from less perfect to more perfect. His contribution to the eastern, particularly Islamic, philosophy is substantial. One of his interesting tenets is that one kind of knowledge is 'acquired' or 'learned' through the senses, and another through intellectual intuition. He also saw knowledge as a combination of the theoretical and the practical and by unifying the two, knowledge becomes not only an informative process but a transformative one too.

This concept of 'acquired knowledge', coming through the senses and another kind of knowledge, which is accessed through intellectual intuition, is an integral part of the Reach Approach. This knowledge that's referred to as 'intellectual intuition', I believe, is a knowledge which can only be accessed by going beyond the senses with such practices as meditation, prayer, introspection etc.

I've spent many years researching what I think is the best that the world has to offer in terms of the enhancement of the human condition and looking at how those philosophies and ideologies can happily co-exist. In Synergy: The Cure for All Ills (the third part of this trilogy) I've gone to great lengths to illustrate how the inner and the outer universes need to truly connect if we are to find wholeness and wellbeing. Otherwise there is the danger that we become trapped either in logic (the head) or in emotions/experiences (the heart) leading to a state of affairs where the two never meet. This subject is covered extensively in the chapter 'All You Need to Know' which clearly demonstrates that theory is never enough. Transformation comes most quickly by finding ways to access these two hemispheres of knowledge and applying what you've learned on the back of that understanding. This is the key to sustainable personal growth.

Another great mind within the Islamic tradition is Shah Wali Allah (1703 – 1762). He lived through a time for Muslims known as the 'Wisdom' period. This was a time of reintegrating and revitalising the study of the Islamic sciences. Philosophy, theology, mysticism and Koranic law were the thrust of his work. His major works were: the Conclusive Argument from God (Hujjat Allah al-baligha) and Full Moons Rising (Al-Budur al-Bazigha). He did go on to write over forty books and treatises. He also served as a religious scholar and spiritual guide, having been influenced by his father (who founded an Islamic institution, a madrasa, in Delhi). He became his father's successor at the tender age of seventeen and this quite remarkable young man began his long journey of shaping and influencing Islamic thought, addressing issues such as: the purpose of creation, the dynamics of human psychology, the higher significance of human thoughts, and the progressive development of human social and political systems. Because of his integrative approach and reconciling of the inner and outer dimensions of Islamic practice he is often compared to the great thinker and mystic Mohammad al-Ghazzālī (1058-1111) who many historians agree is arguably the most significant Muslim after prophet Mohammed.

China also continued to harvest a crop of great thinkers at this time that helped sustain the heritage of their ancestors. Wang Yang-Ming (1472-1529) was such a scholar and philosopher. He, like many before him, had been brought up on the five Confucian classics and had been shaped by the Neo-Confucian educational programme and Zhu Xi's 'School of Principle'. He felt constrained by his education and by the fact that somehow it denied the spirit of the individual. He nevertheless considered himself indebted to his education and background because it had helped him to ask critical questions and undertake the self-evaluation that would go on to shape his philosophical views. Wang is credited with being the guiding light of the 'School of the Mind' (Xin-Xue). This school was characterised by a thorough and severe self-scrutiny, which to a large extent summarised his, some might say, obsession with Self. For him, any person was capable of becoming a sage because all persons possessed an "innate knowledge of the good", since the source of goodness is within oneself and not introduced from outside. He saw 'self love' (a natural expression of the innate goodness) as the basis of all love; love of family, community, creatures and things etc. His legacy (Yang-Ming School) went on to dominate Chinese intellectual history for one hundred and fifty years. This maintained a focus on introspection and self-examination where fault finding was almost literally considered an art. Although his influence had faded by the time of the Ch'ing dynasty (1644-1912) the Yang-Ming School in Japan (Yomeigaku) had a profound effect upon the Toku-gana culture (1615-1867), which went on well into the nineteenth century, and is credited for being a significant intellectual underpinning for the Meiji restoration, which began in 1867.

Another Chinese philosophical giant followed in the form of Dai Zhen (1724-1777) in the eighteenth century. He was an anomaly because the intellectual world of eighteenth century China was a world where scholarship was increasingly based on evidential research. And so the pursuit of philosophy or any attempt to understand the reason and meaning of things was increasingly considered self-indulgent and empty, but this did not dissuade Dai Zhen. He was a brilliant man, well versed in astronomy, mathematics, history, geography, water conservation, etymology (study of the sources and development of words), phonology and rituals. Despite his staggering mind and his extensive knowledge in nearly all areas of human understanding, it was as a philosopher that he most wanted to be remembered. The major works from his extensive history include Inquiring into Goodness (Yuan Shan) and an evidential study of the meaning of terms in the Mencius. He and his work were controversial at the time as he was fearless in his criticisms of many philosophers who had come before him. He clearly was not a follower, but carved his own way. He challenged nearly all that had gone before - even Mencius (371 BC – 289 BC) for whom he had great respect, but whose work he considered incomplete and proceeded to complete it! He went on to redefine the long held concepts such as: 'the way', heavenly way, principles of human nature, human potential and sincerity. He also covered such matters as the relationship of nature to destiny and what is natural versus what is necessary. He encouraged the constructive 'use' of the mind and he saw learning, especially the difficult kind, as food and drink for the mind. For him a truly developed mind has wisdom or 'divine percipience'; it is able to understand the internal texture of things. In other words, a mind capable of seeing things as they really are is able to grasp what is 'necessary' whilst simultaneously observing what is natural. Hopefully as this story of antiquity unfolds, many of the reasons for my respect for the past are becoming ever clearer. I think it is a tragedy for such individuals and their contributions to be stepped over as if they didn't matter when so much of their knowledge, insight and experience is as relevant now as it was then. The concept of a 'developed mind' that Dai Zhen speaks of is a subject I have sought to make more accessible in a piece of work entitled 'The Three Aspects of Consciousness'. This too can either be explored further in Synergy: The Cure for All Ills or you can explore the basic tenets of it on the Reach website (www.thereach approach.co.uk). This is a useful introduction to how one can expand one's perception and experience of the world.

"To a mind that is still the whole universe surrenders."

Chuang Tzu (369 - 286 BC)

CHAPTER 6: JAPAN AND KOREA

What About the Rest of Asia?

As stated earlier in this commentary, I've mainly confined my observations to the two giants of Asia (India and China) as I believe their story is largely representative of the eastern tale. This is also because in truth the story of the rest of Asia would require another substantial piece of work in its own right. However, during the period of history (seventeenth to nineteenth centuries) when the world is getting ready to embrace modernity, it's worth briefly noting some of what was happening in Japan and Korea and some of the historical figures who were key to their philosophical and ideological evolution. Although both countries have their own distinctive cultures, style and beliefs, the areas of overlap in terms of principles and values are quite large and also resonate with the rest of the eastern story.

From the time of Shotoku Taishi (574 – 622 AD), the Crown Prince of Japan, traditionally revered as the sage ruler who led the nation out of tribal division into political unity and cultural greatness, Japan had been largely shaped by

Buddhism, complemented with Confucianism precepts. There has been in its rich and diverse history much questioning and reflecting on 'The Way' (Daoism) and yet the primary themes as in China seem to have changed little for example mindfulness, enlightenment, meditation, rebirth, karma, morality, ethics, poetry as a way to truth, mastery of the ancient texts and respecting the 'Ancient Way'. If one acts with respect for the natural order (heaven), a moral and well-ordered society will automatically follow. These are just a few of the recurring themes. By the eighteenth and nineteenth centuries the Shinto movement (Japan's official religion, which reveres one's ancestry and the spirit of nature) was again trying to reclaim Japan's spiritual past from the foreign ideals, especially Buddhism and the Confucian ideology which it saw as being responsible for overthrowing the 'Age of the Gods' which was enshrined in Japan's past. Here we see another paradox of the past: for on the one hand Buddhism and Confucianism have underpinned so many beliefs in Japan, but at various points in its history they have also been seen as Japan's enemy, having persuaded it to move away from its own past and traditions. This position has been at the core of so much antagonism between China and Japan over the years and yet it has also fostered, for long periods of time, much harmony between them too.

So from the time of prophet Mohammed, Japan has seen a philosophical tug of war between Daoism, Buddhism and Confucianism. Many great thinkers and scholars argued for the virtues of one position over the other with very few seeing the value and the power of integration, so intellectual differences continued to maintain the_a tension between ideologies. This led to different schools of thinking and various sects emerging, each championing a theme or a particular perspective over another. This contributed to the increasing dilutions of these religions and amongst other things played its part in the revival of Shintoism. Shinto (the way of the Gods) had been the native religion of Japan until Buddhism arrived from the Asian continent when its influence gradually fell away. But when two invasions mounted by the Mongol rulers of China (in 1279 and 1281) were both thwarted by typhoons which inflicted great damage on the Mongols, Shinto belief was powerfully rekindled in the conviction that the typhoons that caused the Mongol invaders to retreat and return to the continent were Kamikaze (divine winds) sent by the Gods (Kami) of Shinto. So whereas Buddhism had long been considered to be the protector of the state, Shinto now began to assume that role. This was the first phase of Shinto revival in the early medieval age. The second phase began at the beginning of the fourteenth century during a time when there was dynastic dispute in the imperial family. Discord over succession to the emperorship focused attention on the reviving central myth of Japanese history: the Shinto belief that the Imperial family had been given the mandate by the Sun Goddess, Amaterasu, to rule Japan eternally. Shintoism was re-establishing its belief that Japan was a divine land, superior to its neighbours, China and India. This is because Japan insisted it had been ruled by an unbroken line of sovereigns from its founding by a descendant of the Sun Goddess; whereas China and particularly India were considered inferior because they had often undergone dynastic changes and suffered long periods of disorder without centralised rule. It should be said a written language did not emerge in Japan until the fifth century hence these facts are considered by many to be a myth as they were unable to be verified.

Japan also saw its origins as being of greater antiquity than China due to the genealogy of Japanese Gods. According to Japanese mythology, those who ruled first in Japan were Gods and then came human sovereigns. It was Kitabatake Chikafusa (1293-1354) via his major literary work Jinno Shotoki (Chronicle of the direct descent of Gods and sovereigns) who arguably played the greatest role in reviving the Shinto principles of government, that of ruling from the centre (by a small group of people) and renouncing the Buddhist ideology. Japan at this time had been heavily influenced by the Han and T'ang dynasties and so its social-religious and political views followed the Chinese way.

It is worth underlining that Chikafusa's political - and by default religious - influence did not really make itself felt until later on in Japanese history. But when it was taken up its influence remained strong until the end of World War II. Jinno Shotoki was regarded as one of the principal pieces of literature outlining the ideology of imperial loyalty. Shintoism continued to find its own place as Buddhism continued to re-invent and refine itself within the Japanese borders. It was during this time (twelfth century) that Zen Buddhism was born.

Like the rest of the East, Japan had been scarred by conflict and war, much of which had come from within its own borders, as its many clans struggled for control either amongst themselves or against the emperor of the day. It's out of this 'warring tradition' that the greatness of the Samurai was born, and the idea of fighting and even dying for a principle became strongly revered. In fact, Japan's efficient and effective military position has been conceived out of this long heritage of fighting for a principle, for 'something better'. By 1603 the unification of Japan was achieved and lasted for over two centuries. Ieyasu Tokugawa emerged as master having defeated all his rivals and became the founder of the Tokugawa line of Shoguns. During this period Japan became isolated from the rest of the world as Buddhist sects were broken up and Christian missionary activity was rejected. New laws rigidly defined the role of lords, warriors and peasants and stability and unity was established until 1867).

Korea's Contribution

Korea's story has some parallels with Japan's but obviously it has some unique elements all of its own. From the time of Wonhyo (617-686) in the seventh century Mahayana Buddhism had spread throughout Korea. Wonhyo was an extraordinary scholar who mastered all the advanced Buddhist theories and produced a huge amount of scholarly exegetes (critical explanation of scriptures). He is revered as the founder of the uniquely Korean Buddhist sect (Haedang-jang) and is considered to be the most important seminal philosopher and religious practitioner in Korean history. In addition to his prolific exegetical writings Wonhyo's concern for ordinary people translated into his spending time dancing and singing around the country to spread the notion of joy. He called it Muoe (unhindered). One of his favourite sayings was: "All unhindered persons lead birth and death along a single path" (a passage from the Flower Garland Sutra). His primary message was one of empathy, joy and especially urgency. Focus the mind and don't waste time was his mantra – "Right actions correct the delusions of the mind". "Arouse your mind and practice!" was another of his famous sayings. He evidenced in his own life the need for meditation and contemplation. To him, application was the key. Theory is impotent without practice!

By the twelfth century Chinul (1158-1210) added to Wonhyo's legacy producing many major works of his own such as: Encouragement to Practice (1190) Secrets on Cultivating the Mind (1203-05), Straight Tales on the True Mind (1205), Abridgement of the Flower Garden Sutra, to name a few.

Buddhism continued to thrive during this period of Korean history, having close ties with the royal court. This meant the advice of Buddhist monks was sought on both religious and political matters. There were two dominant schools of Buddhism at the time: Kyo (doctrine) and Son (meditation). However Buddhism in Chinul's time underwent significant reform with the growth of the meditation-inspired form of Buddhism (Son).

It was at this crucial crossroads, in the middle of the Buddhist Koryo dynasty, that Chinul tried to deal with the serious signs of moral and spiritual decline, as the major split between Kyo and Son unfolded. Chinul developed an original approach to Buddhism as a response, in which he merged the speculative metaphysics of the 'doctrine' school with the soteriological (doctrine of salvation) views of Son. This unique integration of Chinul's is considered the most distinctive Korean contribution to Buddhist thought. Korean Buddhists who came later have generally followed the basic principles outlined by Chinul. It was only much later in the twentieth century that his integrationism and attempts at invoking synergy would be radically called into question.

The great contributors that followed such as: Yi T'oegye (1501-1570), Hyujong (1520-1604) and Yi Yul-guk (1536-1584) added to this idea of synergy and in some cases went further. There were of course points of difference but my proposition is that what binds us has always been a stronger force than what divides us! Sadly, our egos help promote a stubborn, often dogmatic view that is unwilling to relinquish the desire for 'being right'. What a price we've paid for that! These Korean philosophers all spoke of: sincerity and single-mindedness, meditation and cultivation of goodness (morality). In fact, Yi T'oegye and Hyujong both believed everyone possesses the potential for salvation and is capable of 'sage-hood', through firm determination, study, self-discipline and right action. Hyujong went further in that he saw the essential teachings of Buddhism, Confucianism and Daoism as the same (on which he wrote a treatise in 1564 called The Mirror of Three Teachings). He suggests that "Confucius planted the root of truth, Lao Tzu then nurtured it and Buddha pulled it out (harvested it)". In other words, all three were and are important, each one being relevant to different parts of the 'unfolding nature' of truth. Yi Yul-guk was a neo-Confucian who studied Buddhism but pursued Confucianism. He became a brilliant philosopher, outstanding educator and dedicated statesman. All three of these thinkers played their part in the evolution of Korean philosophy and I believe most of their propositions are timeless and are as relevant today as they were then.

The overwhelming feel of this chapter of the story is one of great minds rebelling against war and conflict, striving to re-establish the importance of the spirit on the landscape of humanity. Most of the eastern contribution during this time pleads for a metaphysical revolution in which the pursuit of materialism is abandoned, where the ideals of sincerity, kindness, innate goodness, the pursuit of truth, empathy, right action, resolve and self-discipline are prized above all else. It is also repeatedly documented during this period that action is championed above theory, something that I believe has been lost in our pursuit of progress. It now seems that we revere what people know or think they know more than what they do and who they are. Surely we are best defined by our values and how we live our lives and not by how impressive our 'knowledgeable' vocabulary is. After all, does an abundance of knowledge mean anything if it is not usefully and meaningfully applied? Someone who appears to know little and yet lives authentically and with integrity, have they not better understood what is important? Is a mind the size of a planet better than a heart full of virtue? I think not but this is a question you need to answer for yourself.

The events that follow, as outlined in the next chapter, would change the face of the East forever.....

"When I let go of what I am, I become what I might be".

Lao Tzu (604 BC – 531 BC)

CHAPTER 7: MODERNITY ARRIVES

The Role of Introspection?

As we've discovered, the East, just like the West, has been riddled with war, invasion and conflict of every kind. It is also steeped in much hypocrisy and contradiction and yet it has somehow retained a stronger sense of its own 'identity' than is the case in the West. It is a region where understanding of the human spirit continues for many to still be the greatest pursuit. It has been less preoccupied with 'looking out' into the world and has maintained its focus on 'looking in'. Whether it's India, China, Japan, Korea or South East Asia we see this inclination to look within for the answers. Nearly all the eastern religions and traditions cite introspection as ultimately leading to salvation. These traditions would all largely agree that what you see 'outside', is best understood when one is wearing the spectacles of 'insight'. In other words insight is looking at the outside world with the benefit of the wisdom one has gathered from excavating the inner world. Only then can the external world be accurately interpreted and understood. When a person turns their vision (sight) inwards in quiet reflection they come away with the 'information' that the gift of introspection brings. Insight encourages one to interpret what one sees by going beyond logic and the senses. Have we acquired or more precisely developed such insight or do we continue to rely on our eyes and physical senses alone for an interpretation of the world? In India, especially within the yogic traditions, there is much talk of the third eye.... What is this third eye? Does it exist? I believe it does. The third eye is a subtle and highly refined ability, often described as in intellectual intuition (which can be developed through practice). This practice then enhances what one sees when looking out into the world. By taking this road of introspection, through meditation, mindfulness, prayer and spiritual practices, I believe, one is able to find enlightenment, peace and joy.

The Charge of Industrialisation

By the mid-nineteenth century about half the world's population lived in Asia. They were mostly peasants and Asia's industrial activity was confined to hand-made quality goods. By the end of the nineteenth century, half of Asia's population was under European and American rule. It was during this time that Asia was being exposed to nationalistic and democratic ideas, which would eventually bear fruit in the twentieth century and led to calls for independence. There was little native industrialisation during this time as the European rulers had no interest in developing competition from their colonies. Colonial territories were seen as profitable markets and a great source of materials for their own factories and industries.

The industrial revolution brought with it more than technological advancement and change. It brought about complete change for the East. The British, French, Russians and later the Americans and Germans all expanded their empires whilst the older imperialists – the Spanish, Dutch and Portuguese were less active, as they were not at the forefront of industrialisation. This left a few independent Asian states such as: Persia, Afghanistan and Siam, who all maintained precarious existences amidst the huge shifts in power, and empire building. It was China and Japan whose position most changed under the influence of the foreign invaders. The Chinese empire had towered over the majority of Asia for centuries. It was a huge and powerful centralised state, which was undoubtedly one of the world's greatest civilisations. I've not attempted to document here the eastern contribution to the evolution of science as there is far too much to say. This I believe is another tale for another time.

Suffice it to say that medieval Europe had borrowed extensively from Chinese science and technology, which at the time was the most advanced in the world. India contributed significantly too – particularly in astronomy and mathematics in which they were far more advanced. It wasn't until the sixteenth and seventeenth centuries that Europe began to compete and then slowly surpass Indio-Chinese achievements (for those of you who are interested in finding out more about this topic you may want to refer to 'Science: The New God?', part one of this trilogy).

The results of these advancements by Europe were not felt in China until the nineteenth century. Until then, the Chinese emperors had seen China as the principal actor on the world stage. They treated the squabbling European states, who were building their various colonies and empires, as 'bit-part players' striving for central roles in Asia, however they believed they would never attain a lasting foothold. They tolerated Europe's advances as they saw themselves as culturally superior and having invulnerable strength. The Chinese during this period refused to negotiate with the European governments on equal terms. The most they would concede was limited trading privileges on the coast or at the borders.

Japan had been heavily influenced in its evolution by Chinese civilisation but, politically speaking, was a very different state. Its emperor was merely a figurehead and real power lay with a warrior aristocracy headed by a Shogun or Generalissimo. While China had disdain for what it saw as the 'barbarian' world of Europe, Japan was afraid of it. The earlier activity of European traders and missionaries during the sixteenth century had proved unsettling to Japanese society. This is why from the seventeenth century Japan's ruling class forbade contact with the outside world, except for China and Holland (as the Dutch had been more discreet than other Europeans in their trading connection with Japan).

Between 1833 and 1860 Great Britain forced China to abandon her traditional attitude to the outside world and to accept a code of international behaviour convenient to European and American trading interests. As previously stated China was self-sufficient and needed nothing from the Europeans and so British demands were not met until opium became part of the negotiations. It was discovered that China had an almost inexhaustible appetite for opium. By the 1830s over half of the British exports to China consisted of opium, a lot of it smuggled in, as in parts of China it was banned.

Early missionaries recorded the devastating effects of opium on the Chinese people especially in terms of their health, which was very poor. In 1839 the emperor Tao Kuang decided to deal with the situation by destroying the opium to stop its ever-increasing use, but in the summer of 1840, this merely brought about war as the British retaliated. The British at that time had the greatest sea power in the world and the emperor could mount little resistance and by 1842 the opium war ended with the Treaty of Nanking. This was the first of several 'unequal' treaties between China and the West, and it gave British merchants all the concessions they wanted. Hong Kong was relinquished to the British during this period and Britain had access and trading rights to five ports, most importantly Shanghai and Canton. Similar treaties were also granted to the French and Americans. The opium war made it clear that the Chinese could no longer hope to stave off the West. This was arguably the most important turning point in two thousand years of Chinese history, because China was now having to bow down to the French and the British in particular and its premise of invulnerability and cultural superiority had been overturned. By 1858 both France and Britain had gained further trading advantages and their grip on China was strong. Much of coastal China had effectively become a European colony and the Chinese themselves were treated with contempt in their own country, such was the power of the Europeans. For the Chinese, especially the scholarly classes and the now impotent gentry, there was distrust for a civilisation that seemed inferior in every way save for its weaponry! To them, Europeans seemed crude, vulgar and incomprehensible. India was facing a similar fate as France and Britain both sought to expand their empires on the sub-continent. Whilst the Moguls still ruled in the north of India, the south of India became a theatre of war in which the British and the French battled for control (at this time in the late eighteenth-early nineteenth century this was considered the richest place on earth). The Tamil people were the major casualties of these wars, especially as their people tried to resist these invasions but were systematically massacred. They were simply no match for the British who eventually won control in 1799.

This was the first of many conflicts that paved the way for the British Raj. The East India Company that had pursued India merely for profit continued to do so and the 'uneasy peace' simply disguised the fact that the British ambition was to add India to its colonies. By 1857 it did just that. The war in 1857 was seen as the first big battle for independence, which India lost. Up to this point Britain had used some force but had also seduced its way to power through treaties and negotiations. However, by the mid-nineteenth century, Hindus and Muslims stood side-by-side and battled against the British. It was known as the greatest war against an imperial colony, Mangal Pandey. This battle was some twenty-five years in the making and was the result of Indians feeling denigrated by the British. The uprising took the British totally by surprise. The British response to this uprising was staggering. Their brutality was beyond belief. Karl Marx (who was working for the New York Tribune at the time) angrily condemned the British press for not reporting the atrocities committed against the Indians. Marx went on to describe the Europeans as having become "fiends in their pursuit of power". They left Delhi in total ruins and having crushed the uprising they gripped India around the throat – it would be another ninety years before independence on this scale was sought and ultimately achieved in 1947. This latter and successful independence movement was led by three great lawyers, all rather ironically British educated: they were Gandhi, Nehru and Jinnah. It was they who finally led the victorious charge against the British Raj.

So until then, Europe (the West) had China, India and the rest of Asia exactly where it wanted them, servicing its interests and under its control.

During this same period, in the background many great philosophers and thinkers continued to emerge trying to apply reason where it was lacking. Right across Asia the evidence of the 'voice of Antiquity' was struggling to be heard as it pleaded for a kinder, more noble way to be pursued......

Antiquity's Final Plea

Let us listen to those voices in the nineteenth and twentieth centuries, striving in their own ways to prevent us from being consumed by our egos and the spirit of greed. By the nineteenth and twentieth centuries, America and Europe, aided by science and technology, were now the dominant global forces and remain so today – although there is evidence that that is changing with both India and China rising again like 'the phoenix out of the ashes'. Whilst in the grip of colonialism and cultural indoctrination by the West, the East continued, philosophically at least, to fight for its autonomy and beliefs. There were many who played their part in trying to achieve this. India gave us Rabindranath

Tagore (1861-1941) who has been acclaimed as perhaps the greatest literary figure in history. In sheer quantity of work, few writers can equal him. His writings include more than a thousand poems and over two thousand songs; in addition, he wrote thirty-eight plays, twelve novels, two hundred short stories and innumerable essays covering every important social, political and cultural issue of his time. He was awarded the Nobel Prize for literature in 1913, the first such award to an Asian writer. His life-long interest in education led to his founding a school and a university. Not content with being a philosopher, poet, educator, literary giant, songwriter and producer of plays, he took up painting in his old age and became prolific and successful at that too, producing some two and a half thousand pictures. Tagore was a genius and like Gandhi, who was a contemporary of his, the message he exuded in all that he did was love! This principle underpinned his whole ethos and style. He was a truly international figure at the time and in 1915 he was knighted by the British Crown for artistic, social and cultural contribution through his work. However, he later returned the Knighthood, in 1919, as a protest against the British massacre of unarmed civilians in Amritsar. This massacre has subsequently been described as 'the worst atrocity in the history of the British Empire'. Three hundred and twenty-nine people were killed in cold blood and a thousand wounded and General Dyer, the unrepentant officer responsible for the attack, followed it up with public floggings. Though Dyer was eventually dismissed by the British government, there were still many British who vigorously defended his actions, including the House of Lords. The Amritsar massacre helped to give Gandhi control of Congress, which endorsed his view that "co-operation in any shape or form with this satanic government was sinful". And in the summer of 1920, Gandhi began a campaign of non-cooperation.

Tagore's act of returning his Knighthood gives some measure of his overriding view that love and harmony are the very meaning of life and that hatred, injustice and conflict in any form are their enemies. His philosophy and religious views were heavily influenced by the Upanishads. He believed 'true realisation' comes from the love of self, love of family and friends, all humans, animals, trees and God. He believed in 'unity in diversity' and spoke passionately about this in the face of the increasing self-destruction he saw taking place in his lifetime, particularly in the West, which culminated in two world wars. He loved God and nature, believing both to be things of great beauty.

During this same period in India, the Great Mohandas Karamchand Gandhi (1869-1948) was also active. He was lovingly called Mahatma (great soul). Albert Einstein said of Gandhi "generations to come will scarcely believe that such a one as this walked the earth in flesh and blood". His ambition, Gandhi said, was "to wipe every tear from every eye". Although not a great original thinker, what he did has rarely been rivaled. He collected ideas from all religious traditions, especially Hinduism and fashioned a unique and forceful philosophy. He then made his own life the embodiment of his philosophy; he practised what he preached! His greatest achievement was the creation of a new instrument of social action, namely, Satyagraha, also known as civil disobedience. Gandhi learnt the value of tapasya (self suffering or intense efforts) from his mother who was an especially devout Hindu and he learnt religious tolerance from his father who had friends who were Hindu, Jain, Muslim and Zoroastrian (Persian religion founded in the sixth century BC). I won't attempt to tell Gandhi's story here, as much has already been written about him elsewhere. What is relevant to this commentary is that he was a fairly recent example of someone prepared to live and die by his principles. He built his own philosophy on truth and learnt very early of its power. When Gandhi was fifteen he stole some gold to help his older brother. Conscience stricken he made a full, written confession. He had the courage to accept the suffering his actions would incur. His father, after reading the confession, cried and forgave him. It was Gandhi's first lesson in the power of truth and he witnessed its power to arouse love and the power of that love to also reform the heart. This became his template for life and all that he went on to do was governed by truth, non-violence, simplicity and tolerance. Gandhi spoke of and practised the principle "change begins with me; be the change you want to see in the world". He believed being egoless was the highest personal virtue and it was this along with his loving nature that made him so popular and attractive to so many. This is probably why he was able to bring his own brand of spirituality into politics. By 1947 India had achieved its independence through the tenacity and brilliance of Gandhi, Jawaharlal Nehru (1889-1964) and Mohammed Jinnah (1876-1948). These three British educated lawyers were to become the heartbeat of the 'Home Rule Movement' and in spite of their differences orchestrated and engineered the demise of the British Raj in India.

There were other great contributors who played a part in

India reclaiming its destiny, such as Aurobindo (1892-1950), K.C. Bhattacharyya (1875-1949) and Sarvepalli Radhakrishnan (1885-1975).

Aurobindo was a unique politician for he saw Indian nationalism as a return to divinity, India reclaiming its spiritual heritage and then sharing that heritage with the world. Although he had been educated in England and went to Cambridge he became a radical revolutionary who wanted nothing more than to help end British colonial rule in his homeland. Aurobindo had developed a real and lasting love for much of western culture, especially its literary heritage. He was nevertheless faced with the blatant racism and cultural chauvinism of the British attitude at the time. This ultimately is why he vehemently rejected the British notion that they were indeed superior and that colonialism was therefore somehow a 'favour' to its colonies. He went on to help encourage and revive India's belief in itself by pointing to its antiquity, especially its spiritual tradition, which had never really waned despite all that India had been through. Unusually, it was his experiences in yoga that became the vehicle for his political expression and contribution to change in India. He was passionate about integration and as a result created 'Integral Yoga', a system based on the classical forms of yoga of the Hindu tradition (devotion, karma and knowledge), which he combined with meditative and other spiritual practices. He felt this integration embraced the idiosyncrasies of the individual. Integral yoga implied the integration of spiritual practice within the regular activity of life, and so he spent the last forty years of his life spreading this message of integration.

K.C. Bhattacharya was born into a Brahmin family of Sanskrit scholars and as a result from a very early age he was introduced to the ancient Indian scriptures, such as the Vedas and Upanishads. He was very bright and went on to Presidency College in Calcutta. However, due to his unwillingness to appease British administrators, he never secured positions commensurate with his abilities. He held a variety of teaching and administrative positions and retired at the age of fifty-five as Principal of a small college. After retirement he became a professor of philosophy at Calcutta University, then the Director of the Indian Institute of Philosophy at Amalner. Finally, he became the George V Professor of Mental and Moral Philosophy at Calcutta University. He was another integrationist but with a different twist to Aurobindo. Bhattacharya constructed a comprehensive philosophical worldview of his own which was made up of elements from Eastern and Western philosophy. He was well versed in a number of Indian philosophical schools and various Western philosophies, especially Kant and Hegel (German philosophers). What was refreshing about his position is he didn't feel he owed allegiance to any particular school and so he never became concerned with the maintenance or the defense of any particular Eastern or Western school of philosophy: a true integrationist. His philosophy was/is a kind of dynamic system into which new material is assimilated and which then adapts and grows into a new form. His contribution goes a long way towards removing the popular western misconception that Indian philosophy is exclusively mystical, non-rational and unscientific. Bhattacharya produced a substantial body of work on freedom the concept of value and of philosophy itself but his primary focus and contemplation was on the subject of the Absolute, which he addressed in three different phases of his life from 1914 to 1918, 1925 to 1934 and then from 1939 for a period lasting little more than a year. For those who wish to further explore his work on the Absolute, there is much written from each of these periods. For him philosophy is a rational analysis of experience in the sense of conceptual clarification, also the sorting and ordering of epistemological, metaphysical, ethical and aesthetic symbols, all in the name of progress towards the Absolute (God, the universe, perfection). He thought this was best done by marrying Eastern and Western principles, not using them as a basis for division, each striving for a superior position. Far too often intellectual debates on the 'truth' become preoccupied with the 'rightness' of one's position, rather than posing the key question: 'does your perspective inform mine'? Bhattacharya didn't get caught in this trap of the ego and the intellect. He revered truth as the prize.

Sarvepalli Radhakrishnan was India's most eminent twentieth century philosopher. He, like Bhattacharyya was well versed in European and Asian philosophical traditions but his knowledge and understanding went further. He was a world leader in comparative religion and philosophy but he went beyond this as he aspired to be a midwife to the world's 'unborn soul'. His own passage through adulthood reflects some of that aspiration as he rose from professor of philosophy at Calcutta and Oxford to become president of India. He was seen as a master of the English language, a spellbinding orator, dynamic leader and a very generous human being.

Radhakrishnan was brought up and educated in colonial India where Christian missionaries proclaimed Christianity to be the only true religion, portraying Hinduism as being seriously flawed and blasphemous. In his first published works (1923, 1927) he went on to defend the Hindu theory of karma and the ethics of the Vedanta. For Radhakrishnan, karma solved the riddle of evil because it made the individual responsible for his/her own destiny. "The 'agent's' sufferings are the consequences of his own past misdeeds, whether in this life or previous lives". So it's the agent, one's own actions, and not God, who causes evil. Karma however, does not entail fatalism nor negation of freedom. Radhakrishnan, using an analogy from a game of cards, contended that the hand one is dealt is determined by past karma, but the individual is free to play the game as he wishes. This is where free will meets destiny. He also argued that critics of Hinduism were mistaken in claiming that the Vedanta is a body of work advocating a withdrawal from life. He stated repeatedly that, "This world is the field where one enacts the drama of the soul's salvation. This is not done by renouncing the world but by acting in it!" He also stressed that it was imperative that: "One must act to fulfil one's duty without becoming attached to the fruit of one's actions". He saw man's highest path as selfless service and non-violence (ahimsa) and therefore it falls to us all to work for universal salvation.

It is important to note that his first major work, the Monumental Indian Philosophy, was a two-volume history published in Muirhead's distinguished Library of Philosophy series. This was quite a remarkable achievement. It was the first book to present a panoramic view of Indian thought to the English speaking world, especially England where it was widely believed that there was no such thing as Indian Philosophy. He smashed that myth and brought respectability to Indian Philosophy throughout the world. His influence and achievements are too many to list but at this time of loosening the British grip on India, it would be wrong not to comment on what many see as his greatest work: An Idealist View of Life (1932). This is based on a number of lectures he gave in London and Manchester in 1929, known as the Hibbert Lectures. In this work he remarks upon the spectacular success of science in modern times and notes that most current philosophies, using scientific knowledge as a paradigm, recognise only two sources of knowledge, namely sense perception and logic. But Radhakrishnan insisted humans have another form of knowing, which he called intuition (Pramana). He claimed intuition is the fundamental source of cognition (knowing) and provides evidence that the mind functions as a whole. Sense perception and logic were therefore only partial functions of the mind on the one hand. On the other hand intuitive knowledge arises from an intimate fusion of mind with reality, or 'knowing' by 'being' and not through the senses or symbols. Intuitive knowledge, for him, was seeing things as they are, from the viewpoint of a unique individual and not as a member of a class or as a unit in a crowd. Radhakrishnan believed that the 'knowing' which comes from intuition offers a mystical vision of 'absolute spirit', where subject/object duality is transcended, the subject then having the realization that the foundation of the universe is Absolute Spirit, and of the same nature as his/her own deepest self.

Such an experience transforms a person's life and he/she becomes a saint, a seer, or one who has achieved spiritual freedom.

This is a vision that both I and we at Reach share as a result of our own personal and clinical experiences. All things cannot be known or understood by standing on the shores of sensory perception and logic. Be it art, science or morality, our understanding and expression is enhanced by an intuitive platform: this is what Radhakrishnan and Bhattacharya were both encouraging us to explore. They believed the answers to the 'unknown' lay in spiritual and mystical experiences, because it is through them we become one with the Absolute Spirit; and it is in that 'oneness' that the incommunicable can be understood. They did not dismiss other perspectives and philosophical views; on the contrary, they were passionate in their advocacy of religious tolerance. Creeds were unimportant, conduct was everything: through love and righteousness all men will advance to the same spiritual goal. "There are many paths to the same goal and each one should take the one best suited to their individual nature".

In 1936 Radhakrishnan was appointed Spalding Professor of Eastern Religion and Ethics at Oxford University. He was the first Indian and the first Asian to hold a chair at Oxford. See his work 'Eastern Religions and Western Thought' (1939) if you're interested in his best work during that period. From then until 1959, his commentary, writings and other work contended there was one perennial and universal philosophy to be found in all lands and cultures, from the seers of the Upanishads, the Buddha, Plato, Aristotle and Plotinus, Hillel and Philo-Judaeus of Alexandria, Jesus, Paul and the medieval mystics of Islam (Sufis). It is the 'spirit' that runs through the veins of these philosophers and their teachings that can unite the continents and link the ages and save us from the meaninglessness of materialism and the illusions of modernity. He was adamant that human beings need not change the religion they were born into, they simply needed to allow their 'conduct' to truly conform to the 'values' of their religion and not get caught up in dogma. Dogmatic religion relies on authority (force), free religion is based on spiritual experience (power). All religion is a mixture of both but only those operating from a place of spiritual experience exhibit love and tolerance for all.

With the arrival of modernity we can see that India was still a cradle of ideas, values and ethics, nurturing its great heritage and conceiving giants who were busy trying to stem the tide of 'progress'. They could see that whilst there was injustice, inequality, racism and prejudice, what progress was being made was merely an illusion. They cried out for a much-needed spirituality and I too am appealing to those of you who've chosen to read this work to go and find the spirituality in you. Where it is absent, conceive it. Where it is present, nurture it. And at every given opportunity, spread its fragrance through your thoughts, words and actions. Until one's values and ethics are prized above all else there cannot be progress, merely demise. Look into the mirror of our planet, is she not begging for mercy and asking that we change direction now? The responsibility for positive change lives with you and me, so let's choose to make a difference today!

What About The other Giant of Asia?

As India was striving to reclaim its independence, China was also undergoing enormous tension and shifts of its own. Both Confucius and Mencius had a strong sense of mission to rescue China from falling apart, yet neither succeeded: in truth they did not have the opportunities to create such an outcome. However, both attained immortality as great sages and thinkers. On the other hand, Dr. Sun Yat-sen (1866-1925) has succeeded as a political reformer and a revolutionary, yet his contribution to world philosophy has been overshadowed by his celebrated career as a political leader. He was Confucius in action, the founder of new China. His practical principles significantly altered the course of China's history.

Sun was educated first in China then Honolulu in Hawaii, after which he went to Hong Kong in 1884 where he graduated from the Government Central School. From there he then went on to graduate in medicine in 1872, but seeing China's decline and the corruption under the Ch'ing dynasty, he decided to give up medicine in the name of China's reform. He first founded the Society for the Revival of China and travelled extensively in China and abroad to raise funds and recruit members for the Society. In 1905 he became the Head of the Revolutionary Alliance (which later became the Kuomintang or National People's Party). It was here he developed 'the Principles of the People' (nationalism, democracy and 'livelihood' or economics). These principles served as the philosophical foundation for his vision of new China. Sun, together with his supporters in the Revolutionary Alliance, planned many uprisings against the Manchu government in different provinces across China. On October

10th 1911 they finally succeeded. Sun was elected provisional president of the Republic of China but he resigned in favour of Yuan Shikaiwho was the builder of the Northern Army. This gesture, Sun believed, was in the best interests of China but this proved not to be the case. Yuan was not satisfied with the title of President and declared himself Emperor. After a failed revolt against Yuan, Sun left China and did not return until 1916.

On his return he spent the last nine years of his life in continuous revolutions in an attempt to remove Yuan and the residual forces of Imperial China. In 1923 he founded a separate government in Canton. He cooperated with the communists with the aim to defeat the Japanese (who had become China's most recent invaders) and unify China, in order to prepare it for the modern world. Sadly, before his vision could be fulfilled he succumbed to poor health and died in Beijing on March 12, 1925. On April 1st 1940, he was given the title 'Father of the New China' by the Nationalist government. His legacy was substantial, and you can judge for yourself if his vision was achieved. The essence of his ambition was to mobilise China towards democracy, to encourage her citizens to take responsibility by participating in China's destiny. He believed a 'natural inequality' existed, as all humans were not equal in their talents and abilities but he abhorred the idea of what he described as 'artificial inequality'. He saw that as inequality created by kings and lords leading to social injustice and in the end fostering rebellion. Therefore, to avoid unrest or revolution, this 'artificial inequality' should be abolished and democracy put in its place. For Sun, true equality meant 'equal opportunity' for all people – in order that they may maximise their potential without the hinderances imposed by an unjust society.

He saw education as the vehicle for such equal opportunity. To see the differences between Sun's idea of democracy and that of the West, those who are interested could take a look at his 'Five Power Democratic System', which goes some way to demonstrate his political originality. Sun Yat-sen managed in the end to win the respect of all sides in the revolutionary process, which helped transform Chinese society.

Shortly after Sun's passing, during the 1930s, the rise of Mao Tse-tung (1893 - 1976) was to reshape the face of China once more. Mao was well versed in Chinese history and literature and in his early years he was exposed to western ideas too. During the 1930s, aided by translations of Russian Marxism, he became a Chinese Marxist but he was always more Chinese than Marxist in his views. Although not revered as an original philosopher, he was undoubtedly a profound thinker. This is reflected in his reign as the leader of both the Chinese Communist Party and of the People's Republic of China, which lasted four decades. His impact also reverberated around the world. Mao's philosophical influences came from many sources such as: Hegel, Lenin, Marx, Stalin, and Engels - all from the West. He was also influenced by Daoism and the Confucian traditions. His contribution to Chinese thought in the twentieth century includes: "The world is full of contradiction" and dialectics (the art of investigating the 'truth' of opinions by discussion) as the method to handle such contradictions. He also insisted that literature and art were part of the revolutionary machine. Artists and writers should become the "people's tongue and voice". Their work should serve the masses. To do this they needed to study Marxism and learn from ordinary people in order to share their feelings and use their language. He also championed the ideology of 'practice'. This is probably best exhibited in the marriage he orchestrated between Marxism and Chinese traditional philosophy. He wrote a famous piece on the subject called "On Practice" in 1937, in which he explores the relationship between knowledge and practice. He believed this was the formula to unveil truth. He believed through experience a person gains perceptual knowledge and so there is a 'deepening of cognition'. I will come back to this dynamic as it is also central to my work, research, clinical and personal experience and I believe is worthy of further discussion.

Mao's other significant contribution is what he called a 'new democracy', although there are many who would take issue as to whether his concept is democracy at all. Mao kept a Confucian view running through his social and ethical theory, namely that social interests should take priority over individual interests. But he went further; unlike most Confucians he believed in sexual equality – men and women are equal in a socialist society. Therefore equality in all aspects was an imperative.

Undoubtedly, Mao was one of the most influential thinkers in China during the twentieth century but he was also the most controversial. Even his own followers are widely divided on whether he was right or wrong and how much he was responsible for China's successes and failures during his fifty-year domination. The jury is still deliberating his tenure. What is clear is that he brought many useful concepts to the table of discussion and the one 'on practice' I think is of great importance for those seeking positive change. It dares to propose that there is a body of knowledge that is only ever really accessed through experience. No matter how much knowledge one consumes, one is only consuming information. Information provides the 'opportunity' for change but application brings that knowledge (information) to life (experience). And it's the experience that is generated out of that knowledge which enables you to 'see' (know) what comes next in the sequence of understanding…. Back to our friend 'insight' (to see clearly within). This you may remember is a perspective Radhakrishnan, was also championing in India around the same time.

Many others right across Asia were substantial contributors trying to manage the consequences of modernity flooding into the East during the twentieth century such as: Tanabe Hajime (1885-1962), Uehra Sengoku (1899-1975), Nishitani Keiji (1900-1990), Han Yongun (1879-1944), Muhammad Iqbal (1873 - 1938), Sayyid Muhammad Husayn Tabataba'i (1903-1981). It's important to underline that they all, albeit in different ways, encourage spirituality, living more ethically in the world; something that appears to be rapidly slipping away from humankind.

All these great minds and commentators spoke with respect and reverence for antiquity, suggesting that just as the branches of a tree must never neglect their roots or it will wither and die, we too as a race must not lose sight of our origins (roots) or we too will be in danger of stifling or preventing our own growth. Real progress cannot be simply measured in objects, inventions, science and technology. It must include the values, virtues, ethics and morality that are crucial to our emotional and psychological wellbeing....

"A scientific worldview which does not profoundly come to terms with the problem of conscious minds can have no serious pretensions of completeness. Consciousness is part of our universe, so any physical theory which makes no proper place for it falls fundamentally short of providing a genuine description of the world"

Sir Roger Penrose (1931- present)

CHAPTER 8: ANTIQUITY'S LEGACY

What Have We Learned So Far?

I've tried to present what I believe is an invaluable message that has continued to echo throughout history and yet seems to have largely been ignored. It is a true story about the 'voice of the spirit' continuing to speak in spite of the other noises and sounds (war, migration, injustice and religious conflict) trying to shout more loudly and offering their messages through force. The East has been steeped in just as much injustice, hypocrisy and violence as the West. And yet, a different sub-text has continued to persist throughout eastern history. So much so that the notion of 'spirit reigning supreme' still resonates today across most of Asia. It's as if no matter what else has been the subject of re-modelling and change, the principles of spirituality have remained largely non-negotiable. Yes, there been debate, challenge, questioning and amendments to the plethora of philosophies and ideologies but the core concepts of divine consciousness, and of the existence of a supreme spirit have remained largely constant. So too has the need for virtue, conscience, integrity and spirituality.

Despite the various interpretations, as well as the subtle and substantial differences, what binds the East is far more than that which divides it. On closer inspection what we discover is how much conflict has taken place over so little difference! Our egos have seduced us in such a way that we've regularly chosen division over collaboration and arrogance over humility. Look where this position has brought us to as a race... to the brink of our own destruction and what have we really gained?... Progress?... Has it been worth it? Have our scientific and technological advancements given us greater happiness and peace? Are we any closer to the truth? It seems to me that in our desperation to progress we've sacrificed much of what is really important, like empathy, care and compassion for each other, patience and tolerance. Time and time again we've traded in our values and principles, becoming arguably more knowledgeable and clearly less wise! Integrity is now a rare commodity in our 'me-me' society and individualism towers over social conscience, which appears to be rapidly evaporating. The East, however, holds on to more of the things that offer us a way out if we have the courage to let go of the addiction of progress and embrace the 'certainty' of many of the past principles. Let me be clear here, I am referring to the 'certainty' of past principles because I believe that much of what we've thrown away does come with certain guarantees but those guarantees are only honoured when we treat them with the care and respect they deserve. My experience of working extensively with the human condition in a variety of contexts and settings with a multitude of clients and issues has only served to endorse this position further. I believe your experience, given the opportunity, will also do the same for you. However, don't take my word for it. Test these principles from antiquity in the laboratory of your life and see what your own experiments throw up. If you've read this book thoroughly you will have collected many invaluable insights along the way but let me remind you of some that stand out:

1. FOCUS – The mind that is clear and knows where it is going will almost certainly reach its destination. Lack of clarity and focus denies us many of the fruits of success. Developing the art of 'mindfulness' (through practice) opens the door to the heart and gives you access to the unlimited potential of the mind. You'll find these doors cannot be opened with any other key. Focus is about single-pointed awareness, which means focusing on the objective with such intensity that it becomes a 'positive obsession'. Such single-mindedness is irresistible and always wins the day.

2. PRACTICE – having identified what is needed to improve the self, those that apply the 'antidote' again and again …do eventually find relief. Positive change inevitably follows. Practice creates structure, fosters discipline and generates personal power, self-mastery and confidence.

3. DISCIPLINE – 'Practice does indeed make perfect' but without self-discipline the wheels on the wagon of practice become dislodged and fall away. Discipline does not restrain or limit the self, as is often thought to be the case, it sets the

heart and mind free. Those who establish positive routines quickly discover they are carried to their destinations by the momentum that such discipline generates.

4. RESPECT AND REVERENCE – Whether we are thinking about God, a Deity or Nature, the East has a well-established tradition of respecting that which is greater than oneself. Across the diverse cultures of the East there is an immovable belief that there is 'something' that is Supreme and Divine to which we owe thanks. In fact, in most cases, it's considered that it is due to our lack of reverence and respect for the divine force that we generate the negative consequences that reverberate through our lives (the law of karma). For many in the West, the concept of karma remains a contentious issue. But isn't there some validity in the notion that as we sow, so shall we reap? Surely our thoughts, words and actions cannot leave us immune to consequences?.... Look at our planet; is it not mirroring back our mistakes? It seems obvious to me that we've lost respect for life and take things too much for granted.

5. THE ART OF APPRECIATION – An attitude of gratitude is arguably the greatest medicine of them all. There is a well-developed reluctance to complain in the East that would serve the western culture well. Somehow built into cultures of the East is the realisation that complaints corrupt one's vision, spoil one's mind and weaken the spirit. Whereas, appreciation uplifts and heals the mind, body and spirit with its tender caress. I've found through my work and in my own life that the Power of Thank You is second to

none when seeking to rebuild or positively sustain one's life.

6. NON-VIOLENCE – From before Buddha, to the Jains, then the Sufis and more latterly Gandhi, the immense power and value of non-violence has continued to be revered; in spite of the innumerable conflicts, or maybe because of them. This virtue has rarely faded from the spiritual horizon. It is clear to me, that non-violent communication and interaction is the most powerful instrument for positive change we have. Once we understand that it empowers all parties and removes the ego from the debate, we can then scrap the myth that this is a position of weakness and recognise this truly is a place of strength. If only we were prepared to develop the self-control and skills to resolve our differences this way we would surely be living in a better world. Are you ready to take this journey?

7. INTUITION (INNER KNOWING) - The scientific worldview largely scoffs at the idea that intuition is a legitimate form of knowing, as it stands outside of logic and sensory perception and therefore does not meet the conventional criteria for 'evidence'. Is that sufficient reason to dismiss the gift of insight? As you've seen in the East, throughout the ages, many great minds have argued for this form of knowing to be respected as an instrument for probing and delving into the 'abyss of the unknown', so that we may make 'conscious' contact with the truth. My experience is clear, both personal and professional: when one dares to listen and trust their 'inner knowing' an understanding that does not come from any other source is

unveiled. There is a perspective different from logic and from the information gained from the five senses that is invaluable for making sense of the self and of the world. Learn to trust it and watch how quickly it develops.

8. KARMA AND PERSONAL RESPONSIBILITY - Whether one accepts the far-reaching implications of karma or not (i.e. reincarnation and past life consequences etc.), the primary principle of personal responsibility is hard to dispute. The law of karma makes each person responsible for his actions. It invites us to look for change from ourselves first before we seek it elsewhere. It rejects the game of blame and asks us to create the life we ache for by changing ourselves (thoughts, words and actions) in line with our aspirations; for only then can our lives truly honour us. So even if one disagrees with the deeper aspects of karma, it is still possible to embrace its core message: that is, change begins with you…. and what you do will eventually turn up at your door.

9. CONTEMPLATION, REFLECTION AND MED-ITATION – These three activities are all synonymous with eastern cultures and traditions. In fact, for many they are the 'life-blood' of spirituality. Without them one can only pay lip service to personal growth and sustained development. Ironically, scientific evidence continues to mount (in the research around mindfulness and compassion), clearly demonstrating that the mind works best when repeatedly exposed to positive silence. That is, 'conscious contact' with the self, the universe or God. It is in the act of quiet, focused attention that one is able to transcend the limitations of

everyday life and find deeper purpose and meaning.

10. METAPHYSICS – This is an enormous subject that is yet to be given the respect I believe it deserves, even though there are innumerable great thinkers and philosophers either side of the east/west divide who have argued for its validity and inclusion in the human debate. Although they didn't agree on the details, Socrates, Plato and Aristotle formulated clear ideas on this subject and so did Lao Tzu, Confucius and Buddha -some of which I've documented here. In summary, for me, metaphysics encourages one to engage with the invisible forces as well as the visible ones. It's about developing and respecting our relationship with the unseen and not propelling ourselves beyond the natural laws. There is a rhyme and rhythm to life and once we stay still long enough to see and respect it, it has so many lessons to teach us! The question you need to ask yourself is are you really paying attention? Because if not you will miss the unseen forces at work.

This list is in no way definitive, as I could easily have tripled it and still not exhausted these past principles/codes of conduct. Their 'guarantee' of growth is not through hocus pocus or magic spells and potions but simply through the promise that you in the end will always get out what you put in! Consistency generates more consistency; compassion generates care and offers more of the same; being thankful breeds more things to be thankful for. And so although many of these attributes, virtues and values can be charted back to the beginning of recorded history, they remain no less true and relevant today in the twenty-first century. I believe each of these principles/practices would enhance your life and ensure greater peace and happiness.

Antiquity Has Indeed Come Full Circle

I have covered much on our journey and yet I am aware there is so much I had to leave out in order to focus on my primary message. My focus throughout has been more on the spiritual messages that have battled their way through time, trying to be heard by an unwilling audience. I hope you are now listening and can see what needs to be done.

As the curtain is about to come down on this wonderful story, I think it is only fitting to underline Asia's staggering contribution to the world in its current form. There is a whole list of 'firsts' and achievements I've not addressed in the telling of this tale. Below are just a few to illustrate that her contribution is more amazing than most of us would realise. This is largely due to the re-telling of history with an Eurocentric slant in our schools and history books. There is no doubt that the West has made a valuable contribution to history but it's important to note that the foundation of a house is no less important than the roof. I want you to remember for the sake of accuracy that the East built a foundation on which the West was built.

Let me demonstrate what I mean. Here are some 'forgotten' facts that have helped humankind to this point:

1. PARTICLE PHYSICS – is one of the most advanced and complicated branches of modern physics. The earliest atomic theories are at least two and a half thousand years old. In India, almost every rational school of philosophy (whether Hindu, Buddhist or Jain) had something to say on the nature of elementary particles with various schools of thought promoting the idea that matter was composed of atoms that were indivisible and indestructible. So the earliest atomic/molecular theories began to be formulated in India.

2. THE FIRST MECHANICAL CLOCK – was invented by Su Sung (1020-1101 AD). He was a mathematician, astronomer and for many quite simply a genius. It's almost certainly true that had the Chinese not turned inwards, away from the world, then they, along with the Indians, would have led the scientific and technological revolution, given how far ahead they were. When the Jesuit priests brought to China the timepieces the Europeans had invented (in the fourteenth century) little did they realise it was the Chinese who had first invented the clock!

3. PAPER – In the second century BC the Chinese invented paper, using bamboo. During the Sung dynasty (1000AD) they came up with the printed word, which revolutionised the intellectual world and began the information age. This is some five centuries before the West. In the West we are led to believe that the first printed book, which was produced in the fifteenth century, can be seen in the Gutenberg Museum. The Chinese had begun their journey towards the printed word in the eighth century! They were also the first to come

up with printed (paper) money in 812 AD. The first in Europe was Sweden in 1661 and it was 1690 before America followed suit.

4. DIGIT ZERO- As previously stated India is the Mother of mathematics. Were it not for zero, the world would be a very different place. Algebra, calculus and trigonometry also originated in India. The decimal system on which the modern world operates was born there too, a hundred years before Christ.

5. PI THEOREM - In the sixth century, a brilliant mathematician and astronomer, Budhayana, was the first to calculate Pi accurately and explain the concept of the Pythagorean theorem.

6. ASTRONOMIC CALCULATIONS – Also in the sixth century the earliest precise calculations in astronomy were produced by James Q Jacobs Aryabhata (c 500 A.D.). He accurately calculated a number of celestial constants such as the earth's rotation per solar orbit, days per lunar orbit and days per solar obit. Aryabhata was also an amazing mathematician and many of his calculations stood unchallenged for over a thousand years.

7. INSTRUMENTS OF WAR – (Whether it is a matter of pride to be first in this field is another debate). However, the

real point is to understand the East has contributed more to the modern world than it has been given it credit for. By the third century the Chinese had created cross-bows – long before they existed in Europe. These were well-guarded secrets that would not be surpassed until the age of the firearm. It's ironic that the Chinese were the first to invent fireworks (first recorded 512 A.D) as it was a similar science that would become the template for the firearm, which would see them toppled from pole position.

8. PORCELAIN, IRON AND STEEL – China invented porcelain one thousand seven hundred years before the rest of the world. They also, having mastered the secret of heat and the use of furnaces, turned common iron into cast iron and then into steel: another first.

9. MEDICINE - The earliest school of medicine is Ayurveda. Charaka is often described as 'The Father of Indian medicine' but there's a legitimate debate to be had as to whether he is simply the founder of medicine, given his phenomenal contribution to the field. It was he who consolidated the principles of Ayurveda two and a half thousand years ago. His work showed detailed knowledge of anatomy including: digestion, metabolism, immunity, genetics and embryology, to name a few. This quite extraordinary body of work (when you consider the time period) is well documented in various Indian texts, should you wish to explore his work further.

10. SURGERY - Interestingly the father of surgery is also from the East (India). His name was Sushruta. Two thousand six hundred years ago he and his team performed a staggering array of complicated surgeries with as far as we know a high degree of success. Amongst the operations performed were: caesareans, cataracts, brain surgeries, fracture reductions, the creation of artificial limbs and much more.

11. THE COMPASS AND NAVIGATION – The Chinese were the first to invent the compass. These were first only used on land before becoming an essential instrument for sea voyages. In fact almost all maritime inventions came from China, led by their invention of the kite, from which they learnt about wind technology and developed sails – they had done most of this by the second century AD! (It would be one thousand three hundred years before the West caught up with them). The Chinese began using compasses for sea expeditions in the eleventh and twelfth centuries, which eventually overtook navigation by the stars. But by the mid fourteenth century these external explorations ceased as the Chinese began to see such expeditions as an unnecessary drain on their imperial resources and turned inwards. Only merchants and tradesmen continued to roam the seas. It should be said at this point for balance and accuracy, that the art of navigation is said to have begun with the Hindus (crossing the river Sindh), six thousand years ago. In fact the word navigation comes from Sanskrit (considered the mother of all higher languages) – "navagatih", and the word navy is also derived from the Sanskrit word "nav".

12. TAI CHI – The art of exercise and movement. For the Chinese the only thing to fear is standing still! Chi (the life force) keeps the body in balance through exercise. By the first century BC they had worked out many of the principles that along with the Ayurvedic tradition would become the foundation of modern medicine. Tai Chi continues to thrive as an exercise system for balance, health and healing. It understands that movement promotes health and stagnation fosters disease.

I've merely itemized a dozen of the significant contributions of the East (primarily from India and China) and I could have so easily listed dozens more! However, my point is not to boast about the East but to offer proper respect to the enormous contribution the East has made to the world, both spiritually and scientifically. So much of what the West now holds dear started in the East and yet is there any proper acknowledgement and recognition of that?... I don't think there is because I am sure most people will be unaware of much of what has been written here and I believe in part this is why we've lost our way. When we forget where we've come from, proper care of our heritage flounders and falls away as it gets taken for granted. If the branches, leaves and blossom of a tree forget the debt to their roots, bark and trunk, the tree will eventually fade and die. So we cannot afford to overlook and neglect the 'root system' (the East) that has supported the tree of life to this point, otherwise we, the branches, leaves and blossom will lose the opportunity to express our vitality and promise in the world. We then stop acting for the good of the whole and we only see the narrowed and limiting view of the 'I' not 'we'.

It's Time for Change

Despite the best efforts of Gandhi, Sayyid Muhammad Husayn Tabataba'i, Kitaro Nishida, Han Yong'un, Radhakrishnan and many of the great thinkers and contributors of the twentieth century, the East is now showing signs of losing sight of its rich heritage as it battles for its place on the world stage. Often described as the third world or the developing world, its desire to be equal in this age of modernity is there for all to see. China especially is marching to the tune of technology and is progressing at such a staggering pace that many already see her as the next super power. India is also hankering after the time when she too led the world in intellectual pursuits and innovation and as a result there is now growing evidence of progress leading to an erosion of the values and principles she has for so long held dear.

So where to now? .... I believe my point has been adequately made, so I need make no further historical references. My purpose in looking back has only been to inform our way forward. If we compare the place where we stand right now to what has gone before, what are the lessons to be drawn? I believe that a great many have been highlighted in this book, however I will leave you to make your own mind up about the lessons that stand out for you. My openly declared purpose is to invite you to question the premise on which your assumptions and understanding of life are built. I'm inviting you to challenge the 'truth' that informs your outlook, perceptions, values, beliefs and choices and hope that this will elevate you out of any denial, pretence, fear and limited thinking. However, as I wrote in "Science: The New God?" I don't expect or want you to simply accept what is documented here. I am hoping these historical facts and my reflections will catapult you further down the path of self-discovery and spiritual enquiry. Then you can for yourself dismiss or accept what fits into your own examination of the facts. Hopefully you'll trust your own experience too.

As has been illustrated here, real 'knowing' exceeds the boundaries and limitations of logic and sensory perception. We need the kind of 'knowing' which comes from insight and stillness too as a reference because it increases our understanding of the bigger picture. This 'real' knowing offers us so many gifts. Sadly, for the most part we've largely ignored them. It seems clear to me that until we find time for stillness and appreciative enquiry, we will continue stepping over the countless treasures that lie scattered on the floor of our minds.

I hope this voyage has also offered a greater appreciation for those seeking to better understand some of the thinking and rationale behind the Reach Approach. We describe our model in part as a place where "antiquity meets modernity". Hopefully, my exploration of this strand of history goes some way to explaining our respect and reverence for ancient principles. I think many of these principles are needed now, more than ever before - hence their influence in our work. Ask yourself, in the light of what you've learnt here, is there more you could be doing to enhance your personality, character and nature?... Could you in some way improve your contribution to the world?... Is there more you could be doing to enrich the lives of those around you?... If the answer to any of these questions is yes, then I would like to suggest that some of the answers to help inspire and improve your life have already been offered to you on this voyage. Look back again at this narrative, re-read certain parts: there is so much you'll have missed the first time around and with each revision you will learn something new. Your enthusiasm and respect for the past I think will be enhanced and with that an appetite for what you can do with your own life to enhance the future for us all. Please remember, this is not about looking backwards for its own sake, it's about finding the best ways to live going forwards.

I wish you all that you need as you move forward in your life... I hope this work inspires you towards positive change. Don't sit around waiting for a miracle: go and create some miracles of your own!

"An ounce of action is worth a ton of theory."

Friedrich Engels (1820 – 1895)

Peace be with you always....

FURTHER READING

1. Ancient India: From the Origins to XII Century A.D. by Marilla Albanese

2. Ancient India (People of the Ancient World) by Virginia Schomp

3. In Search of the Cradle of Civilisation: New Light on Ancient India by Georg Feurerstein, Subhash Kak, David Franley and Vija Brehanis

4. Tracing Ancient India Through texts and traditions by Nina Mirnig

5. The Cambridge History of Ancient China: From the Origins of Civilisation to 221 B.C. by Michael Loene and Edward L Shaughnessy

6. Three Ways of Thought in Ancient China: History, Philosophy and Economics by Arthur Waley

7. The Philosophy of the Upanishads and Ancient Indian metaphysics by Archibald Edward Gough.

8. The Story of Civilization: Our Oriental Heritage by Will Durant

9. Secrets of the Lost Races by Rene Noorbergen

10. Spiritual Partnership: The Journey to Authentic Power by Gary Zukav

11. The Seat of the Soul by Gary Zukav

12. Tao Te Ching by Lao Tzu

13. A Search for Solitude: Pursuing the Monk's True Life by Thomas Merton

14. Inward Bound by Sam Keen

ABOUT THE AUTHOR

Easton Hamilton is the Director of Reach and the founder of The Reach Approach. Reach is a psychotherapy/counselling and personal development practice based in the UK. This organisation has been running for over twenty years and specialises in all aspects of mental health, self-improvement and in various mind-body programmes. The primary premise of the organisation is that the mind cannot be properly 'fixed' without the needs of the body being met, and the body cannot be properly healed without meeting the requirements of the mind. Easton has worked in the field of mental health and personal development for over 30 years. After more than a decade of working with very challenging issues such as: domestic violence, drug and alcohol addiction, sexual abuse and self-harm, as well as with client groups including: asylum seekers, those fleeing war and violence and those with severe mental health problems, it became clear to him that so much of the help available only managed the presenting symptoms of the client. In fact, each agency seemed to be more bound up with their specialism or area of expertise and so the client/patient or individual striving to find a solution often was overlooked. This was not a conscious or a deliberate strategy; it's just the way social/caring organisations are set up. There simply isn't a whole-person approach or mindset. In many instances it's too time consuming and perceived to be too costly for organisations to work in this whole-person way. It requires much more time and skill and a vision that currently seems to be lacking. This is why Reach was established as an organisation specialising in the whole-person approach, primarily concerned with fixing both mind and body. Out of that desire and ambition a new holistic model has been conceived. This was never the author's plan. It developed as an organic response to the various needs of those crying out for help. The Reach Approach philosophy can be summarized quite simply with the question – why focus on merely putting out fires.... doesn't it make more sense to catch and persuade the arsonist to give up starting them in the first place?

For those of you interested in finding out more about the work that has grown out of Easton's passion to help the individual find his/her answer/s through synergy and integration, please take a closer look at www.thereach approach.co.uk.

Easton and Reach continue to be part of a silent revolution, which concerns itself with the empowerment of the individual through research, education and personal development practices. They are busy promoting the best ways to achieve self-improvement, mindful-living, increased personal awareness and spiritual growth. Easton has consciously sought to not make the organisation's work be about himself because he believes one of the greatest lessons that history has taught us is to remember the message, not the messenger and this philosophy runs through the whole culture of the organisation.

If you have an interest in these subjects, please be persuaded by the message if it makes sense to you and do not to get side-tracked by the messenger.

"A person should only accept a doctrine if his own experience verifies it."

Buddha (563-483 B.C.)

EASTON HAMILTON

FINAL MESSAGE

The East has fought tirelessly to keep a spiritual 'heartbeat' in spite of the force of progress. In fact it could be said that the East's lack of interest in progress is why the West went on to dominate the mathematical and scientific revolutions. This is particularly exemplified with the Chinese advancements in sailing and ship technology. At one point they were leading the world in overseas expedition and trade. And yet they surrendered their advantage in this area because they began to see progress for its own sake as pointless, and so turned inward using their superior knowledge to develop their own culture and dynasties. At this point the West seized the opportunity to develop their fledgling understanding of sailing, wind technology and also expanded trade links, which eventually led to their dominion over the Chinese and the eastern Sub-continent.

The East's attempt to maintain 'a sense of the spiritual' at the heart of modernity sadly faltered because of the conflicting beliefs and egos that kept polluting the pure intentions of those who championed a more divine way of life. This is why the East is littered with countless contradictions, because despite its underlying spiritual endeavour the ego of humankind was repeatedly seduced by the promise of power and control. This is clearly evidenced by centuries of war and terror in the eastern world as it struggled to maintain its spiritual conscience. If you look closely, the West is currently making similar mistakes, allowing itself be lured down so many fruitless paths, in the name of progress.

We are currently on a course of self-destruction. We desperately need to wake up and make changes at every level of human existence. This means: financially, environmentally, socially, politically, emotionally, psychologically and ethically. Without these changes we only have to look to our past mistakes to see what the future holds.

I hope that you have been left with a sense of how critically important it is to prize virtue above knowledge because when knowledge becomes divorced from virtue it can become a self-interested and destructive force, as the story that has been told in these pages bears witness to. What history has shown us is that our pursuit of progress steals something from our humanity, when it is pursued at the expense of those principles and values that we need to hold dear. Is it more important to possess things than to be kind and compassionate? We now stand at a point in the developed world where we seem to have everything and yet it could be argued that we have nothing. Can standing with a basket full of material goodies and yet being devoid of happiness and wellbeing, be said to be a worthy attainment? I think not. It's time to reacquaint knowledge with her ideal partner, virtue. Only then can we enjoy a more certain future.

I also hope you will be inspired as a result of reading this work to ensure that your motives and intentions are now underpinned by the right values. I hope you will now spend time writing a new code of conduct by which you will live your life. I believe, until we all take responsibility and pursue positive change in our lives, the demise of our modern world will continue. We cannot look to others to do this; we have to look to ourselves. As Mahatma Gandhi said: "Change begins with me" and that of course means it begins with you too!

"We are what we repeatedly do. Excellence then is not an act but a habit."

Aristotle (384BC – 322BC)

Printed in Great Britain
by Amazon